For Ellen, Allison and Eric

Preface

Another day of scratching out a living in and around the swamplands formerly known as "The Mule Crossing" had come to a close. Some made money, some had lost and many others made enough to pay their bills with little left over on this hot July day. Tomorrow, the cycle would repeat itself all over again. And it would forever in this inconsequential small town in the Heartland of the United States.

But this night, in the midst of darkness, a late train pulled out of town with guards and their three prisoners destined for a court appearance in the nearby county seat. The train was devoid of regular passengers and businessmen, as most had settled down for an evening in their homes or hotel rooms; most, but not all. For some, their work had just begun.

Within about 10 minutes of leaving the station, the train lurched and the prisoners noticed that something was wrong. First, there was anticipation, then excitement. An unscheduled train stop usually meant an accident or robbery, and since there were no passengers or money safes on the train, their prospects were certainly looking up, for good reason. You see, the majority of their friends were free to carry on about their business and these friends certainly needed the prisoners to plan their next heist. Yes, things were definitely looking up.

The three men in chains strained in the darkness to discern some friendly faces. For a moment, they thought they saw them. People appeared on foot, converging towards the slowing train, rustling from behind trees and through the underbrush. The brakes squealed as the train came to a full stop. Steam rushed out and lingered while the aroma of coal filled the air. Had their friends planned their rescue? The people outside gathered quickly once the train had stopped. Wearing their hoods and carrying lanterns, their heavy coats were turned inside out. It seemed like hundreds of them.

It must have been about this point that the horror finally hit them. There were too many for an ordinary rescue. Sure, they had lots of friends, but not this many. There too many people just to free the three of them. It didn't take that many. Dozens were staring at them in mute silence, crowding the stopped train. The people outside the train had eyes that were wild and bright, illuminated by flickering lanterns. This was no rescue party. It was a mob, a nameless, faceless mob of executioners.

A few boarded the train shouting instructions as the guards stood by in fear, disbelief or as part of a prearranged plan. One by one, the prisoners were forcibly removed from the train. One by one, they were about to be murdered. Nearly a hundred executioners slowly encroached on the three prisoners, kicking and shoving them towards a nearby flatbed wagon. The train was told to leave, which it did without any protest.

An awful silence fell as glaring, illuminated eyes stared at them through the spectral masks. The prisoners resisted, began pleading and demanded to know their fate. When three ropes made their way towards them, they knew. They were lifted upon the wagon. The flatbed chattered, as it was pulled by hand to a massive Beech tree beside the tracks.

Once the wagon had stopped, the prisoners were told they could make a final confession. None did out loud. They had all three fallen silent. At last, one of the prisoners exclaimed

"Confess hell, you've got me here; thousands of you, now do your damndest!"

The mob's patience was over. Nooses were tightened around their necks and the ends of the ropes were thrown over a large overhead limb. The signal was quickly given. The mob began to shout like madmen.

The ropes tightened as the wagon bed slid away from beneath their feet. The remaining moments of their consciousness were filled with shouts and sharp pains and perhaps a last view of each other struggling to remain alive. Their bowels and bladders opened up as they hung. It must have felt like a lifetime.

What followed was a deeper and darker silence. The satisfied mob quickly dispersed in all directions. Few, if any, questions were asked in the days that followed. Few, if any, answers were provided other that three Death Certificates stating cause of death: hanging by person or persons unknown.

This was just the beginning. Within five days, in the same spot under the Beech tree, the mob gathered once again to take three more lives. The mob would strike a third time, fifty miles to the south, raising the death toll to ten. It finally made the National and International news, created an international incident with Great Britain and Canada and resulted in a hastily-crafted Bill in the United States Congress.

Members of the mobs would spend the rest of their lives in denial and self-justification, and so would several generations of their descendants, friends and neighbors. Now the saga is unveiled once again as "Anarchy in the Heartland" tries to explain these inexplicable events. It's a true story you've probably never read about...until now.

Anarchy in the Heartland

Chapter 1: Fortunate Son

Even with a thorough understanding of the conditions at the time, one may still be left wondering why mass lynching occurred and why no one was ever prosecuted. They occurred in Indiana fifty-two years after statehood was granted. It was three years after the Civil War and about ten years before the Outlaws of the Wild West began similar activities many hundreds of miles to the west. The nation was in the process of healing from the War of the Rebellion. Although there were several small pockets of Copperheads or Peace Democrats sympathetic to the Southern cause, Indiana had been a solid Union State. The war's bloody violence had extracted a toll on their lives and additional violence should not have been welcomed. So why did people become so violent so soon after the war? And why was nothing ever about it?

The specific locale was in and around Seymour, Indiana in Jackson County. Seymour is located about fifty miles north of the Ohio River and about one third of the way towards the State Capital of Indianapolis, which had been moved from nearby Corydon in 1821. People primarily from Kentucky and Tennessee had started settling Jackson County around 1813 when the last Native American had been cleared out, in part by General John Tipton. Tipton went on to become Sheriff of Harrison County, Indiana and a major figure in early Indiana politics. The will be more about him later in the chapter. However, it was John Tipton's cousin, Meedy White

Anarchy in the Heartland

Shields, who became the major catalyst for future events relating to the lynching.

Meedy White Shields was indeed a Fortunate Son, but had only three years of formal education. His father, James was part of a large, successful Irish family from Sevierville, Tennessee. James was known as one of the "Ten Brothers" that left Sevierville to resettle in "Indian Territory". Their father Robert had been a noted military man and had built Shield's Fort, or Fort Shields, near Pigeon Forge, though it never saw any battles. Apparently, the large family needed room to spread out and they first moved to West Point in northern Kentucky on the Ohio River at the mouth of the Salt River. One of Meedy Shields' biographical sketches says the family later settled near Corydon, Harrison County, Indiana in 1811, just across the river from West Point.

Of historical significance, Lewis and Clark had recruited James' brother John Shields from West Point in 1804 to join their expedition as a gunsmith, blacksmith and general "fixer". Lewis and Clark later wrote that John Shields performed exceedingly well and deserved special recognition from the US government. John Shields' daughter Martha Jeanette would become the first wife of General John Tipton. The Shields and Tipton families were quite intertwined. So much so, that John Tipton's father Joshua, killed by Native Americans in Tennessee, was married to Jeanette Shields. Jeanette was the lone daughter of Robert Shields, the father of the Ten

Anarchy in the Heartland

Brothers. Suffice it to say that the Shields and Tipton family's gene pool was pretty shallow at a few points in history as were many early American families.

Meedy Shields' father, James, had decided to acquire some new property and was granted about 1,200 acres in Jackson County, north of Corydon. Unfortunately for him, much of the more desirable lands on the southern and eastern banks of a local river had already been claimed. The family moved into the region in 1816. In about 1820, when Meedy was only 16 years old, he found himself in the flatboat business hauling goods to New Orleans, returning via the Natchez Trail. Records are rather sparse, but locally sponsored county histories written in the late 1800s refer to typical cargoes as foodstuffs, pork, nails, etc.,

As one would expect, this was a prosperous activity as Shields bought additional flatboats and remained in the "freight business" for about twelve years. Unfortunately, things had not been going well for his father in Jackson County. There had been a series of legal disputes, as his father grew older. A rival landowner to the north also had about 1,200 acres and either James Shields thought some of it was his, or visa versa. "Malicious Trespass" was evoked in a number of cases that peppered the local court system. The two landowners were battling over property and the motivation appeared to be the acquisition or defense of more desirable real estate; namely rich river-bottom soil closer to the White River. Meedy Shields, himself,

Anarchy in the Heartland

appeared in the Jackson County court records in 1827. He was also sued by his father's nemesis to the north for Malicious Trespass. Something evidently spooked the neighbor into thinking he was losing property to another member of the Shields clan. Perhaps Shields had begun farming or grazing livestock on the neighbor's land.

Shortly thereafter, Shields would take on a greater challenge. In 1832, he enlisted in the Indiana Militia to fight in the Black Hawk War. Black Hawk was a leader of a confederation of Native Americans who did not subscribe to the 1804 Treaty negotiated by William Henry Harrison, Governor of the Indiana Territory and future President of the United States. The Treaty had opened the door for settlements of Native America lands in Illinois, Wisconsin and Michigan. In other words, Black Hawk was trying to make a futile stand against Manifest Destiny. In just a few short months the war was over and new US territories were available. At war's end, Meedy Shields had obtained the rank of Captain and would be proudly known as Captain Shields in Jackson County. A moniker he used proudly.

On August 17th, 1833 he married Eliza P Ewing, daughter of a wealthy farmer from nearby Brownstown. Her grandfather was an Irish immigrant who settled in New Jersey and her father, James, came to Jackson County in the early years that the county was formed. More about the prosperous Ewing family will be discussed later in the chapter.

Anarchy in the Heartland

In 1837, Meedy Shields was appointed as an agent in the county to oversee the disbursement of a $4,000 of excess federal revenue. Later in 1837, Meedy and his brother William M Shields bought two additional parcels of land, 70.13 acres and 58.65 acres as registered in the land office at Jeffersonville, Indiana. Whether some of the federal funds were used for this purpose is not known, but another agent replaced Shields in 1839. This could have been an indication of a problem. In 1840, William was elected to the Indiana State Legislature as common amongst larger landowners, those with political connections and those with capital. Sadly for the Shields family, his term would end in 1841 when Meedy Shields' only brother died while in office in Indianapolis. The circumstances of William Shields' death are a mystery, but there is nothing to suggest foul play. Meedy Shields followed his family's tradition and was elected to the Indiana Legislature in 1846.

When James Shields died in 1847, Meedy Shields received a sizeable inheritance. One could assume that his newfound wealth and landholdings would have satisfied most early settlers, especially those who made farming their livelihoods, but not the ambitious Shields. He bought an additional 40 acres of public land in nearby Bartholomew County in 1851 and 40 more acres in 1852, which was abruptly cancelled in 1853. Bartholomew County's seat of government was Columbus, a town founded by cousin John Tipton in 1820. Some interesting facts surround Tipton and the new town of Columbus, Indiana.

Anarchy in the Heartland

Tipton had built a log cabin on "Mount Tipton" which was really just a small hill overlooking White River that surrounded a flat, heavily forested, swampy valley. The town was first known as Tiptonia, named in honor of General John Tipton. On March 20, 1821, the town's name was changed to Columbus. Tipton was furious by the name change and soon left the area. He not only got mad, he got even. In the early 1850s, Tipton became the Indiana Highway Commissioner and was given the task of building a highway from Indianapolis to Louisville. Upon reaching Columbus, he constructed the first bypass road ever built. The new highway detoured around the west side of Columbus on its way south to Seymour. The cancellation of one of Meedy Shield's land holdings near Columbus in 1853 begins to make sense when the new highway bypassed downtown Columbus and a major financial opportunity may have deserted him.

In the late 1840s, the north-south Jefferson, Indianapolis and Madison railroad had entered Jackson County from the south. Until 1857, its northern terminus was north of the Shields property in an area known as Rockford, named for a rocky ford of stone that permitted easy crossing of the White River. This 900 resident community was in an ideal location and was the largest community in Jackson County at the time. Rail and water transportation were close at hand and farmers and livestock producers alike coveted the rich soil. It was ideal for most except Meedy Shields. While he owned a small gristmill in

Anarchy in the Heartland

Rockford, most of the town's property was on land owned by his father's rival who had taken him to court twenty years prior.

As a member of the Legislature, Shields learned before most that a new rail line was being planned from Cincinnati to St Louis and would cross Jackson County from east to west near his property. The Charter of the new Ohio and Mississippi Railroad Company had been created by the legislature of Indiana in 1848, and amended in 1849 for the inclusion of the legislature of Ohio.

Unfortunately for Shields, the growing commercial center of Rockford was the obvious location where the rails would cross, and that was not acceptable. He could see the financial opportunity slipping through his fingers as his own property values stagnated and his rival's increased exponentially. What was needed was leveraging to guarantee the new east-west railroad crossed the north-south J, M & I line on his vacant property. Shield's land would then become the focal point of the resulting capital, diverting it from Rockford and all the establishments there including a newspaper, doctor's office, Masonic lodge, church, gristmill, pork processing station, etc.,

Shields likely understood that political connections had limited value when trying to redirect a railroad. It would take significant financial and emotional incentives. Money came first. Having bought shares of the new rail line, Shields maneuvered

Anarchy in the Heartland

himself into one of the twenty-one Board of Directors positions for the new Eastern Division of the Ohio and Mississippi Railroad Company. Step one complete. Secondly, the route must cross his property. Enter John Seymour. Seymour was a railroad survey engineer assigned the task to determine the route through rural Jackson County. Under the table money is hard to count, but what was made public was that Captain Shields guaranteed the engineer would have a new town named after him where the rail lines crossed; Seymour, Indiana. As long as the route crossed the good Captain's property, that is. Apparently, Shields did not inherit his Cousin John Tipton's ego regarding the naming of their own towns.

The Shields property where the proposed O&M rail lines would cross was a swamp. The final agreement was sealed by the fact that Shields offered to provide free grading and a 2-mile elevated causeway west of the new town to keep the train above the swamp. In the end, Shields got what he wanted. The new O&M would cross Shields' swamp. Interestingly, the O&M rail lines bypassed the county seat of Brownstown about 10 miles to the west of Seymour. Perhaps this was another result of Shields' behind the scenes negotiations.

The town of Seymour was officially born in 1852. The new train route would cross Shields' land two miles south of Rockford. Unfortunately for Rockford, their residents and businesses were suddenly on the wrong side of the tracks. The only

Anarchy in the Heartland

thing they appeared to have left was the north-south J,M&I train stop continued to stop in Rockford as it had done since the rail lines had been placed. Thus, Shields had one more obstacle to overcome. The J,M&I needed to stop on his land, not two miles north in the town of Rockford. It would take Shields some time to accomplish this final task.

In the meantime, Seymour was platted, lots were sold and cash started rolling in for Shields. The History of Jackson County written in 1886 described it as follows:

"The first public sale of lots in Seymour took place November 11, 1852, and Mr. Shields, the founder of the town, who had nothing to show as an inducement to investment but the project of railroads (on paper) that were soon to come, was most happily surprised at the eagerness of bidders. At that time the ground where the Ohio & Mississippi and Jeffersonville, Madison & Indianapolis depots now stand, was a pond on which water stood nearly all the year, to a depth of several feet. The now well-known Jonas House corner was then the corner of a field, which yielded abundant crops of wheat or corn each year. The greater part of what is now known as the First Ward was a dense forest, which was used as a woods pasture by Mr. Shields, the western boundary of which was defined by a rail fence, running about on the present line of Ewing Street.

Anarchy in the Heartland

A sawmill built by M. W. Shields in the year 1852, and superintended by Stephen Adams, furnished the lumber used in the erection of most of the new houses built in Seymour during the years 1852 to 1855."

Through his legislative and possibly financial influence, Shields introduced a Bill that would require all intersecting trains to come to a complete stop for "safety reasons" or face a stiff penalty. This meant that "The Mule Crossing", as Seymour was originally known, was about to insert itself squarely into the money flowing with the rails. It guaranteed the demise of nearby Rockford; the property values, the businesses, churches, lodges and general livelihoods. A ghost town was about to be born. The Bill was finally enacted into law in 1857. Also in 1857, Shields "persuaded" Dr Jasper R Monroe to stop publishing the Rockford Herald and move to Seymour. Monroe did and began publishing the new Seymour Times. Monroe wrote of this in later years and hinted of worthwhile "incentives" offered by Shields.

The town of Rockford and the primary landholder had been soundly defeated. Shields began to accumulate wealth quickly from the proceeds of lot and lumber sales. The first lot owner was Travis Carter whom later built his own financial empire in Seymour, founding a woodworking factory and a Woolen Mills. Carter would play a major role in future events as they unfolded.

Anarchy in the Heartland

The success of Shields and his associates were quite amazing even by today's standards. He employed his strong will, money, politics, favors and perhaps outright bribery to achieve the goals he had set for himself. The US Census of 1860 listed his estate at about $2 million in current value. It was common not to overstate land or real estate value for the official census so he was likely worth far more.

When the Civil War broke out, Captain Shields had been a Southern Democrat and leaned very strongly to the South despite living in the North. Changing allegiances, he gave an impassioned speech in 1861 to rally young men to form Company H of the 6th Indiana Volunteer Infantry. The 6th Regiment was the first one organized in Indiana and on the morning of the June 3rd, 1861 took part in the first official battle, at Philippi, West Virginia. After the war, three members of Company H would return to Seymour and be forever linked to the gruesome events that would occur seven years later.

Shields was the quintessential capitalist and self-serving politician who prospered far beyond most people of his time. One could celebrate his resourcefulness and may even want to employ similar tactics to garner wealth of their own. But Shields had set events in motion that he may not have predicted nor fully comprehended had he lived to witness them.

Anarchy in the Heartland

Photograph from Middle Creek Methodist Church Cemetery in Sevierville, Tennessee of the newer Robert Shields marker. Robert was Meedy Shield's grandfather. He was a Revolutionary War veteran, successful farmer and patriarch of the Shields Klan.

Recent photograph of Shields Mountain, east of Pigeon Forge, Tennessee. Named after the Shields Klan, this area is now being developed as an exclusive, private community and the area also features luxury rental properties.

Anarchy in the Heartland

Sketch of John Shields Tipton from Who-What-When book 1900; member of the Shields-Tipton Klan of Tennessee, pioneer, early Indiana Militia Commander and US Senator.

Anarchy in the Heartland

Portrait of Meedy White Shields; wealthy Farmer, Capitalist, Militia Captain, Indiana State Senator and Founder of Seymour, Indiana.

Historic Postcard of Seymour, Indiana.

Anarchy in the Heartland

Chapter 2: Children of Fate

Military-minded families like the Shields and Tiptons had advantages over early settlers because of political connections and new land holdings due to their service. It could be argued they were better able to be successful pioneers of Manifest Destiny as it marched westward. At first, the Shields' rivals in Jackson County were no exception. Before the American Revolution, a military family named Reynaud came from the Bordeaux region of France with significant provenance. General Luis de Reynaud served the Duc de Creqy. He had achieved the rank of General during the Spanish wars. Some of his sons left France via England for Stafford County, Virginia and arrived in about 1688. They were believed to be part of a group of Huguenots engaged in a speculative venture. One of these sons was known by his anglicized name of Lewis Reno. By 1711, he had acquired or had been granted about 1400 acres with two partners, most of it planted with tobacco.

When the American Revolution broke out, his son Zeley Reno fought with the Minuteman from Prince William County under General Lafayette and achieved the rank of Sergeant. After the war, he started a large family and eventually found his way to central Kentucky. There was an interesting occurrence recorded in the Cooper's Run Church records of June 15th, 1792:

Anarchy in the Heartland

"After Prayer proceeded to Business Brother Jesse Williams exibited a charge against Brother Zeley Renno, for being at a Logrolling at an unseasonable time, & with drinking to intoxication & swearing, & differing with a Certain Brothiers, & strikeing a Negro. The Church after hearing the Charge and Br. Rennos Defence, are of Opinion that he aught to be admonished and he is hereby Suspended from Communion of the Church until he gives Satisfaction. Done by order of the Church Jas Garrard Clk".

Out of season logrolling aside, during the War of 1812 he served in Demmitt's Company of the Kentucky Mounted Volunteer Militia. It was just before this time that one of his sons, James, left the family and sought out the mouth of the Salt River, near West Point, Kentucky in the same time frame as the Shields. This was likely the result of the Whiskey Trade in the region as discussed earlier. He married Anne Gates in about 1799, and had a son named Wilkinson and five others. James Reno decided to acquire land in the Indiana Territory. One account has his educated wife, was working as a governess for wealthy settlers in West Point. Whether this occupation helped tip off the Renos to new land sales in Indiana is purely speculative, but within reason to assume.

James chose the future Jackson County area and moved his family there in about 1813 before Indiana became a state. He was known to be one of the first white settlers in the area and largest taxpayer in

Anarchy in the Heartland

the county at one time. With this early decision came better property selection. His roughly 1200 acres of land was south and east of the White River and encompassed the area to be known as Rockford. Rockford was named because of the rocky bottom of the White River that provided an easier horse crossing, or ford. Having staked out the area in advance of others, including James Shields, it seemed like his success was guaranteed. By his death around 1843 however, it was probably apparent to him that the Shields clan had sinister plans for the town of Rockford. James Reno's court actions against the well-connected James and Meedy Shields had resulted in little more than fines for both parties.

Wilkinson (Wilkes) Reno, born near the mouth of the Salt River in 1802, married Swiss immigrant Julia Ann Freyhafer about 1835 and had four of his six children by the time he inherited his father's property in 1843. By the late 1840s, Wilkes had become the standard-bearer of his family whether he wanted to or not. His other brothers had either died or left the area. In 1850, Rockford had a Methodist Church, a gristmill, a pork processing station, a Masonic temple, a newspaper and about 900 residents. In 1852, the year Seymour was founded by Meedy Shields, James Reno had six mouths to feed: Franklin (Frank) was born in 1837; John in 1838; Clinton (Clint) in 1842; Simeon (Sim) in 1843; William H (Bill) in 1848 and Laura Amanda (Ellen) in 1851. Wilkes Reno was uneducated and barely able to count his own money according to his son John. John

Anarchy in the Heartland

also wrote that his father was a strong Methodist and insisted the children read the bible throughout the day every Sunday. John Reno also admitted to hating schoolwork and that he and his brothers skipped as often as possible. Wilkes Reno must have been like many fathers and wanted more for their family that he had for himself.

During the rush out of Rockford for Seymour in the mid 1850's, the family was under financial and emotional strain. Farming may not have been Wilkes' passion, but the loss of neighbors must have signaled a deeper problem; loss of hope. Most of his boys had been unmanageable and his relationship with his wife was falling apart. In 1855, John Reno ran away from home on a family horse and made his way to the Jeffersonville, Indiana on the Ohio River. Concerned his son might be labeled a horse thief, Wilkes Reno sent $100 via a cousin to properly pay for the horse and the hope that he would return home. He did not. He grabbed the money from his cousin, boarded a flatboat and eventually made his way to Alabama to see a distant cousin. He returned within a few months and then in 1859, Julia sued Wilkes Reno divorce on grounds of insanity but did not leave him.

By 1860, Rockford was fast becoming a ghost town and the Reno family was coming apart. John's eldest brother, Frank, was living with a common law wife named Adaline Reed in Old Rockford. They listed their occupations as Whiskey Sellers. John lived on the old Reno farm with his younger brothers

Anarchy in the Heartland

Simeon and William, young sister Laura, a cousin Sarah, and a hired hand by the name of McKinney. Julia Reno finally persuaded Wilkes Reno to leave. He took his sons John, Sim and Will and left for Western Missouri and likely road the new Ohio and Mississippi Railroad that had doomed their hometown. After a few short months and apparently not finding work or opportunity, Wilkes and his sons returned to Seymour just prior to the Civil War. He would never live with his wife again and took up residence on Indianapolis Avenue in Seymour.

As the war broke out, politicians and business leaders, including Meedy Shields, made grandiose speeches encouraging young men to enlist in the army. The result of the planned hoopla was the formation of Company H of the 6th Indiana Volunteer Infantry from Jackson County. Frank Reno signed up for a short three month enlistment; it was short because the war was expected to be over quickly. Whether Frank was caught up in patriotism or simply had few alternatives is not known for sure. A large percentage of enlistees viewed the service as a way to better themselves, see the world and learn a skill. Frank Reno was probably looking for new horizons. He left for Indianapolis in April of 1861 and was mustered out in August of that year according to official records. In that time, he became friends with other Seymour residents in Company H, Franklin (Frank) Sparks and Richard (Dick) Winscott. One source claims that Company H was reorganized as Company K of the 17th Indiana Volunteers, organized for three more years and that

Anarchy in the Heartland

Frank Reno had became part of the unit. Supposedly, he deserted the Army in 1863 and returned to Seymour.

Brother John Reno joined the army in 1861, originally with Company H, but was immediately reassigned to Company A of the 13th Indiana Volunteer Infantry. As Frank Reno may have discovered, the enlistment was supposed to be for one year, but reorganized for three year duty. John Reno had been promoted to Corporal and had the rank stripped away for disciplinary purposes. He apparently deserted in 1863 nearly on the same date and in the same general locale as his brother Frank. John and possibly Frank returned to Jackson County in 1863 under a cloud of suspicion since the war was not yet over.

William Reno joined Company C of the 50th Indiana Volunteer Infantry in 1862. The entire regiment was forced to surrender to rebel forces in September of that year, but William was not amongst them. He had gone AWOL, perhaps to avoid capture, perhaps to desert. He made his way through Kentucky, away from the fighting in Tennessee, and took refuge with the Cranmore family. Whilst AWOL, he married a Cranmore daughter in October of 1862 and she convinced him to return to the Army, personally leading him 200 miles to a Union outpost in November of 1862. Shortly thereafter, John C Reno was born. William fulfilled his duty to the Union Army

Anarchy in the Heartland

in the newly organized 52nd Indiana Volunteer Infantry and was mustered out in September of 1865.

Simeon Reno joined Company U of the 79th Indiana Volunteer Infantry in March 22nd, 1865 near the end of the war and fulfilled his obligation.

By 1865, all of the Reno Brothers had returned Jackson County. That year, Frank married Sarah Ford, the daughter of a noted lawmaker from nearby Brownstown. John was working odd jobs on the railroad and scheming. William may have illegally married someone else in Seymour just after the war and Simeon was unattached. The brothers appeared to have convinced their father to buy up the vacant homes and businesses in Rockford with whatever money he had left. Many of the properties had been abandoned and burned. They were bought very cheaply. The Seymour elites had either wanted to seal the fate of Rockford by burning the building themselves, or the Renos had been involved in the creation of bargain prices. But there was another possibility.

The stage was now set for 36 months of chaos. Robbery, mayhem and murder would become commonplace. Perhaps the Reno's new friends who just settled in Rockford had started the wheels in motion. Perhaps the Renos themselves decided to abandon the normal life and become a criminal organization. It is difficult to pinpoint any one event that triggered the violence in and around Jackson

Anarchy in the Heartland

County, but the world would soon read about the horrific events as they unfolded.

After three years, it would finally end with something called the "Night of Blood."

Anarchy in the Heartland

Photogaph from the National Archives of Frank Reno; eldest son of Wilk Reno.

Anarchy in the Heartland

Photograph from the National Archives of John Reno; unbeknownst to him, taken by an old Civil War comrade Richard "Dick" Winscott in a local Seymour saloon at the request of the Pinkerton Detective Agency.

Anarchy in the Heartland

Chapter 3: The Genesis of Anarchy

Seymour had fewer than 1,000 residents in 1860 and by 1862, the population swelled to more than 1500. Their successes, growing wealth and arrogance were made apparent by the following "poem" written about this time:

A FUNERAL ODE TO BROWNSTOWN.

Sadly I view this faded town -
The day is dawning fast
When the old jail will tumble down
And Brownstown breathe its last.

Its officers and cubs at law
Even now seem worn and blank;
Smith wears an elongated jaw,
And Cummins looks so lank.

Poor George's time will soon be out,
Wort certainly soon must die;
And Dan will soon, without a doubt,
See all his type in pi.

Poor Baughman, with his anxious phiz,
Will soon be bound to close;
As also Scott, since flour has riz,
And pork and beer has rose.

Ewing must cease to bustle around,

Anarchy in the Heartland

The railroad now is lost;
Old Peter'll not be always bound
For curses and for cost.

Poor stricken town, with ruined wall,
Waste lot and broken fence,
Receive ye thus the funeral pall
While I go weeping hence.

This prose appeared in "one of the principal county newspapers of the day" according to the 1886 History of Jackson County, Indiana by Brant and Fuller. It is no doubt the work of Dr Jasper R Monroe of Seymour. It illustrates the level of caustic animosity that existed in Seymour towards its rivals which was often espoused by Monroe. It represented what was Seymour's apparent insatiable appetite to devour nearby towns, much to their own benefit.

Monroe had been a paradox in Seymour. He was loyal to the Whigs and against the Democratic Party, yet Meedy Shields was a staunch Democrat his entire life. Monroe was 41 years old in 1865 and a native of Monmouth County, New Jersey. He came west to Indiana and settled in with his family when he was around 6 years old.

Jasper R Monroe had been a Surgeon-Major for the 50th, then 49th Indiana Volunteer Infantry,

Anarchy in the Heartland

appointed by Indiana Governor Oliver P Morton during the Civil War, but left the service early due to an illness. He worked as an editor and publisher both in Rockford, Seymour and later in Indianapolis. Unfortunately for Monroe, Seymour's first recognized doctor had been John Tipton Shields, from nearby Jennings County, Indiana. He was a distant relative of Meedy Shields and the "Ten Bothers" from Sevier County, Tennessee. Monroe may not have been encouraged to open a new doctor's practice in Seymour, but may have seen some patients.

Edwin J Boley, author and Seymour resident researched 12 years and wrote a book titled "The Masked Halters" in 1977 which contained valuable newspaper articles of the era relating to the Reno saga. Only the text of the transcribed articles in italics is contained in this chapter. Additional clarification or commentary was not taken from Boley's book.

On February 23rd, 1865 a front page editorial appeared in the Indianapolis Daily Sentinel reprinted from an earlier article written by the New Albany Ledger. Notice the author's writing style and level of knowledge regarding the details:

"For some months past Jackson County, in this state, has been infested with a gang of daring and bloody-minded villains, whose outrages have at times

Anarchy in the Heartland

been of a most startling character. Robbery and even murder has been committed with a high hand, and so far the guilty perpetrators have escaped detection and arrest. The latest outrage we have heard as being committed there took place on Saturday night last. Three men, two of whom had their faces blacked, and were otherwise disguised, on that night went to the residence of Mrs. Joel Richards, in that township, and whose husband is in the army, and demanded of Mr. R (who was sick in bed.) that she at once give them all the money she had. She told them she had but two dollars which they insisted was dales, and told her that they would kill her and the whole family if she did not give up the money. She protested that she had no other money than the two dollars, when the two who were disguised (the other man standing guard outside with a gun) went to the well and took the tope off the windlass, and dragged Mrs. Richards from the house and hung her up, for a few moments, to a projection from the smoke house. On letting her down, they again demanded the money, which she denied having, and told them she had told the truth. They then hung her again, holding her up till she was nearly dead, and on still affirming that she had no more money, they let her go, and left the premises. This is one of the most inhumane outrages we have ever recorded, and the people of Jackson county should organize a vigilance committee that will hunt down and hang the scoundrels. So many crimes have lately been committed in that county that the people should make common cause to bring the perpetrators to speedy and condign punishment."

Anarchy in the Heartland

The author's name was not published in this early 1865 article that appeared in a rival newspaper in New Albany, Indiana. The next newspaper article of note appeared in the Seymour Tribune on July 27th, 1865. This was written by Jasper Monroe:

"A soldier who had taken a room at the Rader House a few nights ago was robbed of $400, all he had, by some unhung scoundrel, who it appears entered the window from an adjoining roof. Several other robberies were committed the same night. We would advise soldiers and other who are compelled to stop here not to drink, nor to go to sleep, nor to move about unless in sufficient numbers to over awe the gangs of thieves and assassins that infest this place."

"Unhung" appears to infer that the robber deserved hanging. No evidence could be found of a strong public reaction in response to Monroe's gloomy warning. On September 7th, 1865, Monroe wrote about an actual assassination that had just occurred:

"A mulatto man named Granton Wilson was brutally assassinated near his home in Hamilton Township, a few miles above Rockford, by two ruffians about dusk on Wednesday the 30[h]. In company with a colored boy at work for him he had been in search of some hogs. When near his house on the return to men, one a large one with heavy whiskers (probably

Anarchy in the Heartland

false) and the other a smaller man emerged from the woods and inquired if that was Granton Wilson. On being answered in the affirmative they stated they had a warrant to take him to Columbus. Grant replied that he had done nothing to warrant his arrest, but the men were resolve to take him. He then asked to be allowed to go to the house for some clothes, but was refused. He then begged that the colored fellow with him might be allowed to go and bring his shoes. This was agreed to, and when the latter was some thirty yards away he heard the report of a pistol, but feared to turn back. In a second or two four other shots were fired. The family didn't dare to go in search of Grant until the next morning, when he was found on his face, with four bullet holes clear thru him from the back, and his hands clenched in the grass. It appears that Grant ran when first fired upon, and thus receiving the other shots to the back. The negro boy heard him cry, "Oh, Lord!" It seems that Grant knew the men, for he called one of them by name, but his companion was so frightened that he forgot the name.

Wilson has been in the army some time. He was engaged with certain white men in the robbery of Gilbert's store, and the post office in Jonesville some two years ago. He turned State's evidence. The case is still pending in the U.S. District court, we believe, and the whole matter hung on Wilson's testimony. In addition to this he was privy to and probably an accomplice in most of the robberies, house burnings and counterfeiting enterprises perpetrated hereabout

Anarchy in the Heartland

by the gang of desperados that have given Rockford and unenviable notoriety for years past. And the belief now going around that the testimony of colored witnesses will be taken in any court at no distant day afforded sufficient motive for the murder of one in possession of such important secrets. Interested parties are suspected and will probably find it hard to escape the vengeance of the law."

Monroe was wrong. No one was ever identified, nor any grand jury investigations launched. Perhaps one less criminal was suitable for the local authorities and Wilson was a person of color. Case closed. This must have been an embarrassment for Monroe who asserted that justice would be served.

On or about September 29th, 1865, William E Mower from Monroe Township in nearby Jefferson County was apparently returning from being mustered out of Company D of the 4th Indiana Calvary in Indianapolis a week before. This statement conflicts with as federal documents claiming he was mustered out on June 29th in Edgefield, Tennessee. Regardless, he found himself staying in Seymour for the night. He supposedly set out on foot sometime after his arrival to visit some family members about 2 miles north of Rockford.

Once in Rockford, Mower was apparently approached by a group of about a dozen young men.

Anarchy in the Heartland

He was taunted, ruffed up and challenged to escape, which he ultimately failed to do. They found him nearly unrecognizable with his skull beaten to a bloody pulp the next day. On October 12th, the Seymour Tribune proclaimed the following:

> *"Three of the parties implicated in the Murder of William E Mower were before Esq. Carter last week, but by some species of legerdemain only one witness for the prosecution appeared and this was not a very material one. Plenty more were in town, but justice as administered in Seymour didn't require their presence. The investigation will be resumed tomorrow but will probably amount to nothing. It is a fact that should be known that any crime from theft and arson up to murder may be perpetrated in this place with perfect immunity, provided the perpetrators have a little money to bribe lawyers. No man's life nor property is secure in this place. We have no law, or at least no justice. But in these remarks we are not expressing any opinions as to the guilt or innocence of the accused. The principal actors in the tragedy are at large, and will probably remain so.*

Monroe was right, no one was ever charged in the murder. It was about this time that Monroe had probably given up on a legal solution for the growing problem. On October 25th, 1865, a rather common crime brought out another harshly worded Tribune

Anarchy in the Heartland

editorial. This editorial would become the genesis of the vigilante mantra:

"The Jewelry shop of Mr. G. Williams, in the Post Office, was "cleaned out" by burglars early Sunday morning...The letters of the Post Office were not disturbed, which seems to indicate that the rogues are Andy Johnson Democrats. They were young men with good eyes, also, because they rejected the spectacles. The people will pretty soon be ready to act upon the frequently repeated suggestions of this paper, to organize bands in self-defense against the organized bands of thieves and cut throats that infest the country. Nothing but Lynch law will ever be of the slightest avail. Let a public meeting be called, a vigilance committee be formed and the place made too hot for thieves. Every man who has property in Seymour, or who feels and interest in its property, should assist in expelling from the place and county all idlers, gamblers, and others who have no visible means of support. No such person should be permitted to stay an hour in town with his neck out of a slipping noose."

Apparently, the deaths of Wilson and Mower were not a major tipping point for Monroe, as his most forceful editorial to date was issued as a result of stolen jewelry.

Anarchy in the Heartland

The paradox of and educated and intellectual Dr Jasper R Monroe is perhaps no better explained that his editorial which appeared in the Seymour Tribune on November 2nd, 1865:

"Sam Dixon who was engaged in the robbery of Gilbert's store in Jonesville has just been sentenced to the penitentiary for four years. It will be remembered that this was the robbery case in which Grant Wilson was a witness, and upon whose testimony it was thought the case would turn. He was therefore killed as related in these columns a few weeks ago. But the Court and Jury took the recorded testimony and the evidence of two witnesses who swore to what Grant said in his testimony were all the time be, and convicted the accused thereon. So that his murderers didn't make much. This goes to show how hard the irrepressible nigger is to get rid of. Even though dead, he speaketh - yea even in court where the Democracy wouldn't admit him while alive and in full possession of his own peculiar odor. Others engaged in this robbery are still at large."

Monroe takes obvious delight in the conviction of Dixon for the robbery, but obviously made a crude joke about the fact that Granton Wilson had already given written testimony to the authorities and others corroborated it. It seems like Monroe's attitude towards people of color were not far removed from his

Anarchy in the Heartland

sworn enemies, the Southern Democrats. It seems he had little remorse for Wilson's murder.

By late December, 1865, if the residents of Seymour had hoped for a happier new year, they would be sadly mistaken. 1866 would be one of the worst in their short history.

Anarchy in the Heartland

Regimental banner of the 49th Indiana Volunteer Infantry where he reportedly "used liquors and went on sprees". Monroe quit 6 months later.

Sketch of Oliver Perry Morton; Indiana's Governor commissioned Dr. Jasper Roland Monroe as Surgeon to Cyrus Dunham's 50th Infantry. Monroe complained and was reassigned on March 11th, 1862. He then resigned his commission on August 4th, 1862.

Anarchy in the Heartland

Chapter 4: Fear and Hope

On January 3rd, 1866 a young man from nearby Medora, Indiana goes missing while visiting Seymour. He was about 24 years old. Woodmansee was heading to Cincinnati via the rails for business and decided to spend the night in Seymour to await the morning train. Monroe made a brief mention of what happened next in the Seymour Times:

"Mysterious Disappearance - Much apprehension is felt for the safety of Moore Woodmansee, a merchant of Medora in this county. On the 3^{d} inst. he stopped here on his way to Cincinnati to wait for the morning train, passing at 4 o'clock. He left Mr Holmes auction store, then in the east part of town, a little before 9 o'clock, to go to the Rader house, to bed, since which nothing has been heard from him, He was known to have a large sum of money about him, which gives color to the dears of his friends that he met foul play, and probably his death here."

Not long after Woodmansee's disappearance in early 1866, a tragedy of another sort rocked Seymour. Meedy White Shields had died unexpectedly on February 6th, 1866 of "acute stomach trouble". He was laid to rest in the City Cemetery, where his father had originally homesteaded in Jackson County. Monroe' Seymour Times article was surprisingly abrupt:

Anarchy in the Heartland

"We expect this week to be able to give some extended remarks upon the public and private character of the distinguished gentleman. But we are still crippled in our company force, and must be brief. Capt. Shields was in many respects a remarkable man. We always regarded him as a man of great ability and force of character. All that prevented him from becoming one of the foremost men of his party, (for he was a politician by nature) was the want of an early education. His ability was of the practical kind. He had no theories. Any problem he couldn't work out he dropped. Nearly his whole life was spent right here. His business transactions reached almost every man in the community, yet he was never engaged in litigation. Mr. Shields was respected by all and honored and loved in his own family. He was twice elected to the State Senate. Mr. Shields was born in Sevier County, Tennessee, July 8th, 1805 and was therefore in his sixty-first year at the time of his death. We sympathize with the bereaved relatives at the great and irreparable loss."

Though Shields had bargained for Monroe to leave Rockford, Shields had been a lifelong Democrat and that fact placed him opposing Monroe in ideologies and politics. Monroe wrote a graceful piece, but made an incorrect statement about litigation. Meedy Shields did have problems with the Reno family as did Shields' father, James.

Anarchy in the Heartland

In reflection, Shields had just over a decade to accumulate wealth and create his town by the time he had died in 1866. He had used any means necessary to achieve the goals he had set for himself, but one wonders about the price he ultimately paid. Acute stomach trouble could have meant cancer or ulcers, brought on by stress or alcohol, for many people lived beyond 61 years of age in 1866. His father had lived to be 78 and his mother Penelope White (whose father's first name was Meedy) lived to be 73. Shields days appeared to have been shortened by his lifestyle and choices. Sadly, his wife Eliza lived a little over 9 months longer and died in November 9th, 1866 at the age of 59. Both of the founders of the town of Seymour were now gone and there was great sadness, but also a power vacuum.

Another tragedy occurred in nearby Medora. On February 22nd, 1866 the Seymour Times reported:

"Shooting at Medora - Mr. A. W. Flinn a well known citizen of Medora in this county, was shot and killed on Monday by a young man named Emery. There had been some difficulty between them and it is said Flinn threatened to kill Emery before he left town, and remarked to Emery that he should leave on the next train. On hearing this Emery drew a pistol and fired four shots, killing Flinn almost instantly. Emery gave himself up. Flinn was a man of shrewdness and fine address, but he was suspicioned of being engaged in counterfeiting and the Deputy United States

Anarchy in the Heartland

Marshall was on this way to arrest him when he got the news of his death. On his person were found $2,100 in counterfeit money and $100 in good money. These are the particulars so far as we have been able to learn them."

What this appears to indicate is that a respectable citizen had become in the lucrative business of counterfeiting money. This had been nothing new, as John Tipton bragged about clearing out the counterfeiters from Harrison County as early as 1812. But apparently Jackson County offered a home for the new era of criminals. There is little doubt that the Renos were involved in counterfeiting to some degree and may have been a focal point these illegal activities.

In May, Travis A Carter used some of his growing assets and bought into a large Woolen Mill Factory, It initially employed about 40 people, which was a large manufacturing concern for the time, but apparently the Renos wanted no part of it.

Seymour's new Town Marshall was elected in May, by the name of George Slagle. He resigned a few weeks later and Richard Winscott was elected to fill the vacancy. Slagle was about 30 years old in 1866 and a native of Ohio. He was a carpenter by trade and probably sensed that he was not the right person for the job. He remained in Seymour as a "Bridge Carpenter" in 1870.

Anarchy in the Heartland

Richard "Dick" Winscott was not only a contemporary of Frank Reno, he served with him in Company H of the 6th Indiana Infantry along with Reno Gang member Frank Sparks. This put Winscott in a difficult position with his old army buddies and may have signaled that the Reno Gang could continue their crime spree.

John Reno had been in Illinois for part of 1866 when a strange story hit the Seymour Times on September 13, 1866:

"John Reno of this county, and George Mace met with rather rough treatment at the hands of the Mayor, Marshall, deputy Marshall and home citizens of Pana, Illinois, a few days ago. Mr Goss of this place had a valuable horse stolen some weeks ago. He was in Pana in search of his horse, Reno and Mace being there arrested on suspicion, and locked up. In the night the officials above named, with some unknown men, all in disguise, took them out of the jail and deliberately hung them till they were nearly dead. The hanging was done to extort a confession, but both men persisted in their innocence. Reno was strung up five times till consciousness was gone. Fifteen minutes elapsed the last time before he came to. The men constituting the mob were drunk. The next day the Mayor, and Marshalls were arrested, found guilty of an attempt to murder, and refused bail, but a mob rescued them from the Sheriff. Mace and Reno were then brought here for trial on a charge of the

Anarchy in the Heartland

Governor. They were heard and acquitted a few days ago by his Hon. Mayor Greene."

Pana, in Christian County Illinois, was a small town very similar to Seymour. It had been founded in 1845 at the intersection of two major rail lines, just like Seymour. Apparently, the Renos did not strike fear in the town officials as they did in Seymour. Perhaps it had something to do with the "liquid courage" the good Mayor and his Town Marshals enjoyed before their official interrogation of the prisoners.

The next day, Christian County Sheriff stepped in to enforce law and order. Shortly thereafter the good citizens of Pana rescued the Mayor and his renegade officials from the Sheriff. During this time, the prisoners were shipped back to Seymour where the Mayor cut them both loose. No mention was ever made if poor old Giles Goss of Brownstown ever found his horse after traveling all the way to Illinois to find it.

Jasper Monroe must have been fuming at these turns of events. First, one of the Reno boys finally gets thrown in jail out of state, then nearly killed, then brought back to town. Only to be released by the Mayor of Seymour. Monroe must have felt that John Reno had nine lives and nothing he could do or say was going to change anything.

George Greene was a bachelor from Pennsylvania and tailor prior to becoming Mayor of Seymour in 1864. He was about 64 years old in 1866

Anarchy in the Heartland

and most likely was looked upon as an elder statesman. He had been the Mayor of Seymour since its incorporation earlier and it appears the Renos had no fear of him, nor did he of the Renos. Perhaps it had all been a big misunderstanding by that wealthy rich farmer from that troublesome town of Brownstown.

Summer had been winding down in Seymour with the crisp air urging the trees to explode into their spectacular fall colors. While there had been much to laugh and cry about in the first ten months of the year, there had also been some real progress made by the wealthy class. Monroe was not entirely disappointed with the state of affairs.

A new Woolen Mill had been constructed, in part by Travis Carter. A new county agricultural fair was organized for Jackson County in Seymour, not Brownstown. Meedy Shields' sons Lycurgus L. and William H. had constructed a new dam on the White River and built another gristmill, founding the new town of Shields. The boys took their father's cue and located it two-thirds of the way towards Brownstown from Seymour on the O&M rail line.

In addition, a new horse track was built just north and east of Seymour which gave many locals something to do in their spare time including the Renos, since betting of any kind was reported to be one of their favorite pastimes. And a new road, now called US Highway 50, was under construction. This major highway would eventually span 3,000 miles and

Anarchy in the Heartland

link Ocean City, Maryland and West Sacramento, California.

Despite the loss of their founder, 1866 had been a benchmark year for the town of Seymour founded in 1852 and officially incorporated in 1864. As thoughts turned towards the autumn harvest, Seymour had every reason to be optimistic about the future. Then on a fateful evening in early October of this promising year, their world would be turned upside down. The events in the waning months of 1866 would send shockwaves reverberating throughout the county, the state, the nation and finally the world. No one at the time could have ever predicted it.

Anarchy in the Heartland

Early 20ᵗʰ century photograph of downtown Medora, Indiana, home of Woodmansee and Flinn. Both were some of the earliest victims of violent crime in Jackson County.

Photograph of a Civil War monument and cannon in Shields Park, Seymour, Indiana also taken in the early 20ᵗʰ century. Shields donated the land to the city of Seymour before his death in 1866.

Anarchy in the Heartland

Late 19th century photograph of the original Pana, Illinois railway depot. Like Seymour, Pana had bisecting railroads. Perhaps this made the John Reno feel right at home.

Photograph of John Hedding Blish, Meedy Shield's son-in-law, had access to capital and formed the prosperous Blish (flour) Milling Company in Seymour, Indiana. Blish came from a family of millers in Vermont and was on his way to the California Gold Rush when he took a railroad job in Jeffersonville.

Anarchy in the Heartland

Chapter 5: The Autumn of Grief

It was Saturday night, October 6th, 1866 about 6:20 PM. The stores in Seymour had closed and the saloons remained open to cater to the thirsty travelers and locals who were beginning to enjoy a raucous Saturday night on the town. Other than a few saloons, brothel and train depot, Seymour was just about closed for business, but not quite.

The evening train on the O&M was arriving and began to slow for its normal stop in Seymour. As the evening sun lit the platform, two unidentified men approached and quickly climbed on board the train as it was departing. Perhaps the men had approached any other waiting passengers and told them not to take this train. Just as likely, there was no one else traveling at this hour. Steam hissed, a bell sounded and the engine chugged. The train was headed eastbound towards its next major stop in Cincinnati.

The new riders sat in the forward-most passenger car, quietly waiting in the night's gloom as the Seymour disappeared behind them. Unnoticed, pulled pasteboard masks out of their coats. One was white and the other black. Heavy navy pistols were strapped to their waists. About two minutes after departure, the men left the passenger car and made their way towards the front of the train. Their destination would be the Express car, two cars behind the engine. It was strictly off limits to passengers. This

Anarchy in the Heartland

particular Express car was owned and operated by The Adam Express Company headquartered in Boston.

They opened the forward passenger car door and briefly stepped out into the cold darkness with the countryside flying past them. Without light, they struggled to maintain their balance between the shifting cars. The men made their way to the rear platform of the express car. They opened the door. An Adams Express Messenger, named Elam B. Miller, saw them. One of the hooded men drew his gun and demanded to be taken to the safes. Miller momentarily froze at the sight of three ghostly figures aiming their pistols at his head. He slowly complied, more confused and bewildered than angry. The world's first train robbery began at approximately 6.30 PM on a rainy evening of October 6th, 1866 just east of Seymour, Indiana.

The leader of the robbers waved his pistol and ordered Miller to open the safes. Miller reached for his keys, fumbled with lock and eventually opened the smaller safe. The "local" or "way", as it was called, contained all the valuables such as mail, legal paperwork, packages, money and coins that each town was shipping out that day. The robbers stashed as much as they could into their pockets. There was no time to sort through the papers or count the money. There were people waiting in the darkness down the tracks.

When the loot was stashed, the leader demanded the through safe be opened. The "through"

Anarchy in the Heartland

was a larger and more valuable safe that carried more valuable bank to bank transactions to and from the bigger cities. In this case, it was St Louis connecting with Baltimore, New York or Washington DC to the east. Whatever the final destination for the through safe, the robbers knew the contents would be several times that of the local. Time was running out. The robbers manhandled the safe towards the side of the car and opened the loading door to the chilly night air. Then they pulled the brake line.

Surprised by the brake alarm, the engineer slowed the train. There was no time to question the reason for the alarm. The safe was pushed out the open door. It hit the ground with a thud and began to tumble. The robbers jumped from the slowing train but not before pulling the brake line twice to signal an all clear to the engineer. The world's first train robbery was over about fifteen minutes after the train left the station.

It would take many years before a newspaper would write a detailed story based on interviews of Adams Express detectives, Hazen and Egan. On February 19th, 1878, the St Louis Republican wrote this story about the immediate aftermath of the robbery:

"The route agent, who happened to be on the train upon reaching the next station procured a handcar, and with others went back to where the train had been stopped, and, tracing the safe, in which the $38,000 was, found it about seventy-five yards from the

Anarchy in the Heartland

railroad track in the woods, untouched. The night was rainy and the ground rather muddy. On Sunday Mr Hazen was telegraphed in Cincinnati, as was also Mr Egan from St Louis and both met at Seymour on Monday morning. They were not long in getting on the trail of the course taken by the robbers, which was to the house of Wilkes Reno, the father of the Reno family.

The parents of the Reno boys did not live together; the father lived on a small farm a short distance from Seymour, and the mother near Seymour. John Reno was for a short time a brakeman on the O-M Railroad, where he learned the use and management of trains, which afterwards helped him so much in his calling.

Next day, Tuesday, being election day at Seymour John Reno and a man named Frank Sparks, and Sims or Simeon Reno were at the polls and betting largely on their candidate, to the extent of nearly $1,500. In the meantime, Hazen and Egan ascertained that John and Sims were seen boarding the train on Saturday night at Seymour. They watched John, Sims, and Sparks closely that day, and having before then obtained the impression of the snow prints of the three men who left the train, with the contents of the safe. And comparing them with those of John, Sims, and Sparks made that day at the election polls, they had no doubt as to their being the persons.

Anarchy in the Heartland

Warrants were sworn out, but so great was the terror in which in which the Renos were held that no one could be found to execute them. Hazen and Egan and the two others with them constituting themselves as officers, waited their opportunity till the arrival of the train going west, and finding John Reno standing on the platform secured him, by picking him up suddenly and putting him on the train. Sim, who had been drinking, followed John into the car to ascertain what the matter was and only knew his own situation when a pair of spring cuffs bound his wrists.

After this, Sparks was readily arranged, and the train started. Reaching the county seat, the detectives and their prisoners were put off. Next day search was made of old man Reno's house, and in the room occupied by John Reno was found a pair of pants torn on the knees, two coats, all mudded and wet, the two masks, one black and the other white; and two large navy pistols, somewhat mudded, a large quantity of stolen property, the proceeds of several burglaries committed in the neighborhood. Between the ceiling and garret were found a lot of moulds for making counterfeit half and quarter dollars; also several jimmies and burglar's tools, skeleton keys, etc."

All were arranged for hearing at Brownstown, the county seat, but waived examination, giving bonds in the amount of $15,000, John's having been put at $8,000. Indictments were found by the grand jury and bail given."

Anarchy in the Heartland

It's interesting to note that the law in Seymour would not execute the warrants that railroad police Lawrence Hazen and John Egan invoked. This did not dissuade the private security force; they simply kidnapped their suspects and ransacked Wilkes Reno's home. By this time, the loot from the robbery appeared to have made its way back into the local economy with gambling on horses and the election. For now, the robbers made bail and were free to carry on about their business.

On October 29th, eight year old Caleb Hackman was walking near the White River, several miles downstream from Seymour and spotted something on the bank. Upon closer inspection, it turned out to be human remains. He quickly summoned help. It was apparent to those arriving that the victim had not died of natural causes. There was no skull and ample evidence to believe the victim had been beheaded. The headless corpse was not likely the work of scavengers. This was a clear case of murder with sinister intentions far beyond simple robbery and disposal of a body. Beheadings, or similar mutilations, certainly were indications of violent retribution.

Because of the time in the water, the remains were badly decomposed and offered few clues to its identity. Other than a body without a skull, there was only one identifying characteristic, a deformity in the bones of one of the feet. Fearing the worst, Asher Woodmansee arrived. Woodmansee tearfully

Anarchy in the Heartland

confirmed that it was his son, who had been born club-footed. At long last, Asher Woodmansee found his son, dead and decapitated. He would never know who killed his son or why, and would die himself within a decade brokenhearted. There was no Coroner's Inquest.

On November 13th Eliza Shields, widow of Meedy Shields, died at the age of 59. She had lived only about nine months after the death of her husband. Eliza was widely regarded by most townspeople and was a devout Christian. While Meedy was not known to be religious, Eliza had promoted religion vigorously and helped found the local Presbyterian Church. She had been stricken with partial paralysis in about 1856 and this undoubtedly contributed to her early demise. The founding family of Seymour had now officially passed into history, leaving the next generation to carry on. For all the hard work and effort the Shields put forth to build Seymour from scratch, it's ironic they only lived a little over a decade to enjoy the fruits of their labor and see their town grow. Both had died well before their time.

November passed without further incident and so did most of December. On a cold winter night, just four days after Christmas, another senseless murder occurred in Jackson County. In Owen Township northwest of Brownstown, Marion Cutlor had lived alone. She had been reported to be senile or partially insane because of her eccentricities. Around midnight, two men broke the door down to her cabin. They

Anarchy in the Heartland

found her sitting upright in her bed. One of the men put a pillow over her head, pushed her backwards, tore open her nightgown and raped her while the other was rifling through the house. She was then raped again by the other robber who eventually strangled the hapless widow. Marion Cutlor lay dead.

1866 had been a bad year for Jackson County. Their dream of a peaceful life and prosperity had been under attack for many months. The outside world was beginning to read about their crime problems and their reputation was being ruined. Jackson County was on the verge of economic and social collapse. Desperate, the citizens looked towards the state government to fix the problems. It wouldn't take long for them to give up hope.

Anarchy in the Heartland

Photograph of Civil War era steam locomotive and wooden passenger cars not unlike those used by the Ohio & Mississippi Railroad during the reconstruction period. Seymour's trains usually had 6 to 7 cars. Reportedly, the O&M used the Niles Locomotive Company's steam engines.

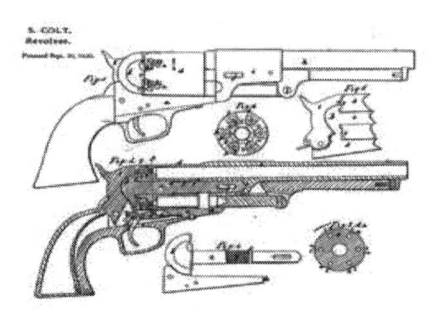

The original patent sketch of Samuel Colt's 1850 revolver. Colt made a fortune selling this weapon during the Civil War. The Reno Gang was said to have favored the Navy version of this handgun and used it during the first train robbery.

Anarchy in the Heartland

This is the only know photograph of Frank Sparks from the National Archives. This was the right half of the photograph taken in the saloon with John Reno for the Pinkerton Detective Agency. Army buddy Dick Winscott strikes again.

Anarchy in the Heartland

Chapter 6: Chaos Arrives

Concerned neighbors found the body of Marian Cutlor sometime in January and the horror quickly spread through Jackson County. Several citizens came forward and told of strangers around the area in the hours before the rape and murder. This lead to several suspects being named. Monroe's Seymour Times carried this piece on February 7th, 1867:

"One John Brooks living in Washington County who as arraigned as one of the participants in the murder of Maria Cutler (sic) near Clear Spring, this county on the night of December 29th, was a few days ago taken to Clear Spring to give evidence against esp. Jackson Easton, arrested upon the same charge. Brooks, it seems under the impression that a conference on his part would result in acquittal, owned up, and gave Easton and one John Talley a brother in law of Easton, as his accomplices in the murder and robbery. Easton and himself are now in the Brownstown jail. The story of Brooks is that the robbery was concocted at the house of Easton, near that of the murdered woman. That Easton showed them the way, but didn't go with them; and that on parting with them charged them not to hurt the woman, and only to get the money."

Most local historians agree that Talley and Brooks had no connection with the Reno Gang, other than their crime was committed in far western Jackson

Anarchy in the Heartland

County. Easton was a Kentuckian who had moved into Jackson County a few years earlier, Brooks was from Washington County, Indiana to the west and Talley was from Illinois.

On February 14th, the new Jackson Circuit court in Brownstown was finally in session and a Grand Jury indictment was issued for John Reno for grand larceny of Charles Mark's watch and chain on September 11, 1866. The next day, the robbery indictment for the October 6th heist was issued for John and Sim Reno and Frank Sparks. Witnesses included Egan and Hazen. Then on February 19th came the indictment for John Talley and John Brooks for murder in the first degree of Marion Cutlor. Two other indictments against Brooks and Talley for robbery were issued; one of them included Easton as an accessory.

The first case in front of the court was on February 22nd. This was the Cutlor robbery indictment that included all three parties. Each entered a plea of not guilty and the case would be continued. Later in the day, the Judge read the case against John Reno for larceny and ordered the indictment filed without calling the defendant to enter his plea.

Afterwards, the Judge called Talley and Brooks to the court a second time for the first degree murder charge. The defense lawyer, Cyrus Dunham, entered a plea of not guilty for both Talley and Brooks and made a request for separate trials for each. The court

Anarchy in the Heartland

awarded Dunham this legal maneuver and the prosecuting attorney, Robert Weir, motioned for a continuance a trial date was not set pending agreement by the attorneys and the court. Talley, Brooks and Easton could not make bail and were returned to the Brownstown jail to await their fate.

Finally the same day, February 22nd, the Judge called the Renos and Sparks to the courtroom for the train robbery. They pleaded not guilty. The trial was set for the August term of the court. They all posted bonds and walked freely out of the courtroom. There is no doubt the people of Jackson County were dumbfounded by the apparent ease of the Reno Gang making bail and set loose to freely roam for six more months. All it took was a few thousand dollars, collected by family and friends and the presumptive train robbers were free.

Without a doubt, there was fear that the same legal maneuvering and slow adjudication could free Talley and Brooks, if they could get enough money to bail out of jail. The citizens of the county waited for several weeks for a new hearing to be set. They waited until the early morning of March 31st. One of the better accounts comes from Dr Jasper Monroe's Seymour Times on April 4th as to what happened next:

"On Sunday morning about 3 o'clock John Talley and John Brooks where hung to a tree in the court house yard in Brownstown. It will be remembered that these men robber, outraged and

Anarchy in the Heartland

murdered a lone and partially insane woman named Marian Cutlor, living near Clear Spring, in this county, on the 29th of December last. Indictments were found against them, but their trial was postponed, and the usual steps taken by the mercenary and unprincipled lawyers, headed by the notorious Dunham, to defeat justice. Esqr. Jack Easton who is also implicated in the horrible affair, was to poor to satisfy the heartless rapacity of the lawyers, and so was prepared for trial, at the late term of the circuit court in Bedford, a change having been granted him.

But we believe the State's attorney wasn't fully ready, and he is yet in jail at that place. If he had been at Brownstown Saturday night the State would have happily been rid of further trouble with him. And so of Cyrus L Dunham. The crowd called for him, and we are assured if he had been there that no power would have saved him from suffering the fate of Talley and Brooks. The people fully understand that it is the lawyers who thwart justice – that but for their readiness to espouse the cause of criminals, and to share with them the money got by highway robbery, arson and cold blooded murder of the unsuspecting and unoffending, these crimes wouldn't be committed.

The robbers and murderers have confidence that the lawyers can and will clear them. They know that money will buy exemption from punishment. Let it come to pass that no lawyer of influence can be bought to the defense, by foul and villainous means, of notorious criminals, and crimes will become less

Anarchy in the Heartland

frequent. There is little difference between the lawyers who, by all rascally means attempt to defeat justice and to acquit the criminal whom he knows to be guilty - who pocket part of the blood-money - there is little difference between his guilt and that of the murderer he defends, and both should meet the swift justice meted out to the hardened wretched by the noble men who met at Brownstown Saturday night.

And it will be done now, of some of them don't take warning. When a lawyer goes beyond securing to his client, by fair means, and impartial trial, he becomes confederate in the crime. Talley had made over valuable real estate to Dunham, and was to give him an enormous fee, contingent, it was understood, upon an acquittal, but we can't vouch for the contingency clause in the contract. The people feel a conviction that the law no longer offers adequate protection to persons not property. And this conviction is well founded. And hence the people are fully justified in defending themselves as best they can against men banded together for lawless and murderous purposes.

While the country is full of lawyers too lazy to work, and who must live by their wits, it will be full of thieves and murderers. Each class is necessary to the other, and the destruction of either one will be the death of the other. The thief and murderer for gain can't pursue his avocation without the lawyer, nor can the lawyer live and thrive without the patronage of the thief and murderer, or other lawbreaker.

Anarchy in the Heartland

This story of this visitation at Brownstown is quickly told. About 9 o'clock Saturday night it became known that a large number of men and horses were about the old fair grounds, near town, nit their purpose was mere conjecture. These were men from Washington county and he eastern and southern portion of Jackson. It seems that another division came in from Owen and Salt Creek townships. The crowd was under strict discipline, had its officers and was duly sober, quiet and orderly. The men were not disguised, and no attempt was made to avoid recognition. It is sufficient to say that many of the best citizens of the county were active participants. The number was near three hundred.

After the jail was surrounded a demand was made for the keys, but this was peremptorily refused by jailor Edmonds and Sheriff Scott. A sledge hammer was then procured and in a few minutes the door was battered down. Tally (sic) was given time to write a letter to old acquaintances, and told some of them that he had never harmed them. He was cool, and showed no signs of fear. He said he was in their power and only asked to be hung like a man.

Arriving at the court house yard, with the rope around his neck, he pointed out to them a better tree than the one they had selected. He consented to have a minister called to pray, but said he was innocent of the murder of that woman. The crowd showed the greatest respect, taking odd their hats during prayer by Rev. Walter Benton. Am man ascended the tree and

Anarchy in the Heartland

fastened the rope to the limb. He asked them not so shove him off, and he then leaned forwards on the rope until he swung off. It is too bad to see a brave man thus sacrificed. But when talents and courage are directed to robbery and murder the possessor must abide the penalty.

Brooks was terribly agitated, and begged for his life. He offered to confess everything, and to give the names to companies of men banded together for illegal purposes from the Ohio to Indianapolis. But his denial last court of his previous confession and his well known character for lying, caused the crowd to put no faith in nor care anything for his confessions, Tally had hung about five minutes before Brooks was strung up by his side. Indeed it looked at one moment as if his life would be spared, it being suggested that he was a mere fool, and a cry being raised to spare him. But those immediately about lifted him from the ground, and the man in the tree swiftly fastening the rope he was left dangling in the air. He died harder than Tally.

The bodies hung about three fourths of an hour, when the men mounted their horses and rode off. Before leaving they took a vote as to whether they should hang some men accused of a theft in the southern part of the county last simmer and now on bail. The vote was unanimous to hang them. They also resolved to wait until next court for Easton to be tried, but if his trial was not then had they agreed to hang him, and will do it.

Anarchy in the Heartland

A citizen of Brownstown was visited and informed if he was caught in any more dirty tricks he would go the way of the others. Anxious enquiries were made for Dan Mitchell (colored) who some of them (from a distance probably) understood was guilty of a murder. Other suspected persons were inquired for. As the work is at last begun it is pretty certain that it will be continued until the country is rid of thieves and cut-throats and till honest people can move about without being knocked down and robbed, or can go to sleep with some assurance that they won't be murdered before they awake.

In the past two years we have had in this county numerous thefts, several revolting rapes, and six brutal murders; and Tally and Brooks are the only men yet punished.

It should be clear to any reader that Monroe's article was more of a manifesto as opposed to a journalistic report. Also, the wealth of detail in this piece would make one think the author was there. These two sentences appear to be a first person account:

"Indeed it looked at one moment as if his life would be spared, it being suggested that he was a mere fool, and a cry being raised to spare him. But those immediately about lifted him from the ground, and the man in the tree swiftly fastening the rope he was left dangling in the air. He died harder than Tally."

Anarchy in the Heartland

The epic battle between good and evil was now underway in Jackson County. Soon, it would be difficult to tell them apart.

Anarchy in the Heartland

The Jackson County Courthouse as it appears today, this is the site of the old jail and the hanging of Talley and Brooks. Both were interred on the grounds for a short period, when rumor had it, Cyrus Dunham had the remains exhumed and shipped to New York.

Cyrus Livingston Dunham served as Colonel in the 50th Indiana Volunteer Infantry. He had been elected to represent Indiana's 2nd and 3rd District from 1849 to 1855 in the United States Congress.

Anarchy in the Heartland

Chapter 7: 1868 – Anarchy in the Heartland

Rather than editing and rewriting the dark events of the year 1868, the History of Jackson County written in 1886 provides a remarkably level-headed report of the recent events:

THE "RENO GANG"

A history of Seymour would be far from complete without more than a mere allusion to the dark days of 1865 to 1868, inclusive, and the scenes of lawlessness that were enacted in and about the town during that period.

Situated at the junction of two great railways, connecting fourof the largest Western cities, namely Cincinnati, St. Louis, Louisville and Indianapolis, it was of easy access to the camp followers, thieves, counterfeiters, garroters and confidence men who gathered at all railway centers to entrap the unwary soldier returning to scenes of peace.

Here, too, was the home of the long famous - or infamous - Reno gang, whose daring feats of robbery have taken front rank in the pages of the criminal history of our country.

Frank Reno, the recognized leader of the gang, was the oldest of five brothers; three of whom met their deaths at the hands of a mob; another has but

Anarchy in the Heartland

recently begun his second term in prison, while the fifth has at all times been adjudged innocent of crime. The family was reared on a farm near Seymour, and, previous to the latter days of the war, were highly respected and prosperous. Frank was a strange compound admixture of good and evil, the latter trait predominating. Among his neighbors and every-day associates he was very popular, was strictly honorable in business transactions, and more than once he gave warning to friends of impending robberies about to be perpetrated by some of his associates. He was tainted with that dangerous doctrine of the communist, whose chief tenet is that the rich may be robbed with impunity, having more than their share. Perhaps, to the end that his conscience might find relief, he distributed a part of his ill-gotten gains with a lavish hand among the needy of his native town.

It is the generally accepted belief that the Reno brothers themselves took little or no part in the petty robberies, burglaries and other thefts that were of almost nightly, and sometimes daily, occurrence from 1864 to 1868. They were, no doubt, however, cognizant of what was going on in that regard, but confined their personal operations to more prolific fields. Numerous bank and county-safe robberies, which took place in various parts of the country, during the period named, were, without doubt, their work, or that of some of their more skilled confederates.

Anarchy in the Heartland

EXPRESS ROBBERIES

Marshfield, an isolated water-station, is situated about twenty miles south of Seymour, on the Jeffersonville, Madison & Indianapolis Railway. Here, at 11:45 on the night of May 22, 1868, while the engine was taking water, the engineer was surrounded by half a dozen men, one of whom knocked him down, while another presented a pistol to his head and threatened to take his life if he uttered a sound of alarm. The fireman shared a like fate. The robbers then uncoupled the combination baggage and express car from the train, and all were disengaged, getting on board; the engine with the baggage and express car were run northward. After passing Austin, the first station north, they forced an entrance to the car, overpowered the messenger, and broke open the safes. They were rewarded for their work in the capture of $90,000 in new notes. On nearing Seymour they halted, and, leaving the engine and car on the main track, dispersed.

Some eighteen months previous, a train on the Ohio & Mississippi Railway was boarded when a short distance east of Seymour by three robbers, said to have been John and Simeon Reno, and Frank Sparks. The messenger was knocked senseless, and after rifling one safe containing some $15,000, the other, containing $30,000, was rolled from the moving car. The robbers in this instance being close pushed, the safe and contents were recovered intact.

Anarchy in the Heartland

In December, 1867, Michael Collarn, then it mere boy, and Walker Hammond boarded the Ohio & Mississippi train near the same place, and, under almost similar circumstances as related in the foregoing paragraph. They secured $8,000, but were recognized and were soon after arrested. Previous to his arrest, Hammond was decoyed to Rockford, two miles north of Seymour, through a message from a dissolute woman of that village, and, while on his way at night, was set upon by one of his companions in crime and robbed of his share of the booty. Both himself and Collarn were sent to jail, where they baffled the law for a time, but a plea of guilty and a sentence of seven years each finally saved them, no doubt, from the terrible fate that was meted out to so many of their companions by the vigilance committee.

The last of the four great attempts at express robbery, which went so far to give Seymour an unenviable name, was not only not successful, but it proved most disastrous to the gang and was destined to be the beginning of the end of outlawery in this region. James Flanders, an engineer on the Ohio & Mississippi Railway had by some means gotten into the good graces of the robbers, and they counted him as one of them, though he was by no means so regarded by the community. The plot to rob the train at Brownstown was hatched and Flanders agreed to render them all the aid in his power. The plan was that they should come upon him unexpectedly, at the water station, apparently overpower himself and fireman, and uncouple the express car as was done at

Anarchy in the Heartland

Marshfield. The attempt was made early on the morning of July 10, 1868; the programme worked perfectly to all appearance at first. The car was uncoupled without the least alarm being given and the engine and express car moved swiftly eastward with six robbers on board the former. After going a few miles, the engine was halted in a lonesome spot, and the robbers made a rush for the express car and forced open the door, being eager to finish their work. Flanders had secretly notified the authorities, and six guards, armed to the teeth, were ready to receive them. This was a most grievous surprise to the robbers; but the guards acted indiscreetly in opening fire before the robbers could get into the car.

The result was, that after a short resistance, the robbers beat a hasty retreat and escaped, all but Val. Elliott, who received a severe wound in the shoulder. The, engine and express car were returned to Brownstown, and the train went on its way to Cincinnati, where Elliott was placed in jail. The other robbers proved to be John Moore, Charles Roseberry, Frank Sparks, Frelingheysen, Clifton and Henry Jerrell. In the surprise and shooting from the express car, Sparks had a finger shot away, and Moore received a wound in his side.

The news of the attempted robbery was soon made known, and in less than an hour a squad of thirty men started in pursuit of the robbers. After a long search, Clifton and Roseberry were found and captured in a dense thicket near Rockford: they were

Anarchy in the Heartland

at once heavily ironed and conveyed to Cincinnati for safe keeping.

JUDGE LYNCH'S WORK

Whatever the opinion of the casual reader may be, the residents of Seymour and vicinity at the time of which this history treats, felt that they were justified in taking steps to check the lawlessness which worked as a menace to honorable trade, rendered life and property insecure, and offered an example for the rising generation which must ultimately result in ruin. The recognized law being found inadequate, through the manipulation of the leaders of the gang, whose stolen money was found an even ready means with which to influence juries, witnesses and prosecutors, the law of might was appealed to. A vigilance committee was organized in the ranks of which were the majority of the best and most trustworthy men of the city and county. A brief summary, to follow these details, will enable the reader to judge whether or not the extreme measures they inaugurated for relief were justified.

Ten days after the attempted robbery of Brownstown, July 20, 1868, Roseberry, Clifton and Elliott were taken on board a train at Cincinnati for the purpose of being conveyed to Brownstown, where a preliminary hearing was to be given them. The train and prisoners passed Seymour unmolested, but two miles west, the engineer was brought to a sudden halt by a red light vigorously displayed before him. As soon as the train halted a crowd of masked men entered the

Anarchy in the Heartland

train and demanded the three prisoners, calling them by name. A slight resistance on the part of the guards was ineffectual, and Elliott, Roseberry and Clifton being taken in charge by the mob, the train was signaled to move on. The train had been halted at the mouth of a narrow lane. A beech tree stood by its side some 200 yards distant from the railroad. Here the prisoners were halted and told that their time had come. A few minutes were given them to prepare for eternity. Roseberry maintained a dogged silence, Elliott was defiant and Clifton begged in vain for mercy, declaring his innocence to the last. Soon the word of command was given by the leader, ropes were hurriedly placed about the necks of the three wretches, and, at a second command, they were launched into eternity.

So quietly was the work done that a German farmer living but a few rods away was not aroused. Next morning he was horrified to find three stark and stiff bodies dangling from a tree almost at his door. He promptly gave the alarm, and after a coroner's verdict of strangulation by parties unknown, the bodies were allowed to be taken charge of by relatives.

THE SECOND HANGING

It will be remembered that Frank Sparks, John Moore and Henry Jerrell were concerned in the attempted robbery at Brownstown. They were in the thicket near Rockford when the pursuers were pressing them, but escaped and made their way by rail and on

Anarchy in the Heartland

foot to Coles County, Ill. Here, being out of money, they went to work as farm hands, though two of them were suffering from painful, though not serious wounds. Jerrell had a sweetheart at Louisville, and, unknown to his companions, wrote to her, detailing his distress and that of his friends, and soliciting an answer to be sent under an assumed name. Of course every friend of the outlaws was shadowed by Pinkerton's detectives, who were employed by the Express Company to hunt down the guilty parties. The young woman, being illiterate, asked a second party to read the letter, and the reading was over heard by a detective. Two days later the three were arrested, and on their way to Brownstown jail via Indianapolis.

The south bound train from Indianapolis to Seymour was late, missing connection with the night train west on the Ohio & Mississippi Railway. There being no place of safety in Seymour the officers having the prisoners in charge determined to convey them by wagon to Brownstown, eleven miles distant. A wagon was at once procured in which they were placed, heavily guarded. Having to pass under the very tree on which their companions were hung but a few days previous, the prisoners were naturally uneasy until beyond that point, when they manifested relief.

Their rising spirits proved without warrant. When some 200 yards beyond the fatal tree there arose, as if from the ground, a crowd of men numbering at least 200, all wearing masks. The wagon was promptly surrounded and halted. The guards were

Anarchy in the Heartland

ordered out and placed under guard of a detachment of the Vigilance Committee; the driver was ordered to "right about face" with his team and load, and was again brought to a halt under the hangman's tree. Here Jerrell, Sparks and Moore met a similar fate to their three companions in crime, with no witness to their awful fate save those who were sworn to secrecy.

THE NEW ALBANY TRAGEDY

Thus far the Renos had escaped the vengeance of the mob. Simon and William Reno were under arrest and in New Albany jail, charged with participating in the Marshfield robbery. (It is proper here to state that many believe William Reno, who was not more than twenty years of age at the time of his death, innocent of the charge which cost him his life.) Frank Reno and Charles Anderson, accused of the same crime, were at Windsor, Canada, well out of the law's reach. Under a solemn pledge of Mr. Seward, then Secretary of State, backed by promises of the express company which had been the sufferer, that Reno and Anderson would be granted a fair trial, a writ of extradition was secured, and the two prisoners were brought to New Albany jail to await the action of the court in Scott County, where the crime was committed. Here on the early morning of December 12, 1868, Charles Anderson, Frank, Simeon and William Reno were taken from their cells, presumably by a band of men from Jackson County, and hung until dead from the stairway of the jail. The details of this tragedy are too well known to need repetition.

Anarchy in the Heartland

Let it suffice that the sheriff and turnkey, Mr. Fullenlove, now dead, made every resistance in his power. He was severely wounded in one arm by a shot from one of the band, and his life was threatened in vain, that he might be induced to give up his keys. His wife, at last, to save him, imparted the desired information, when the mob found ready access to the cells.

Thus was ended the career of the chief outlaw, his companion, Anderson, and his two younger brothers. Clinton Reno, who, as before stated, was never accused of wrong-doing, was a farmer by occupation, residing near Rockford when the tragedy occurred. He is now a prosperous merchant of a Western town, and throughout all he has maintained a reputation for honor and integrity among his fellowmen.

John Reno, who was next in age to Frank, was found guilty of burglarizing a county treasurer's safe in a town in Missouri, and sentenced to the penitentiary for twenty-five years. He began his term about one year previous to the hanging of his brothers. He served ten years and ten months when he was pardoned by Hon. B. Gratz Brown, then governor of Missouri. He was rearrested at the threshold of the prison on the charge of participating in the second mentioned express robbery. On reaching home he readily procured bail of $20,000 through the instrumentality of well-disposed persons, who believed that himself and family had been sufficiently punished for their misdeeds.

Anarchy in the Heartland

Soon after this the case against him was dismissed, and he was once more a free man. He engaged in farming, which he followed with indifferent success for about five years. But the old liking for crime returned, and in the winter of 1885 he was arrested on the charge of passing counterfeit money. Some months later he entered a plea of guilty, and was sentenced to the northern Indiana penitentiary for a term of three years and three months.

A correspondent of one of the leading daily papers, writing soon after the New Albany tragedy, summed up the other crimes happening in and about Seymour, during the four preceding years, about as follows: Moore Woodmansee, a merchant of Medora, twenty miles west, while on his way to Cincinnati, having on his person $2,800, took lodging at the Rader House, then the leading hotel in Seymour. After retiring to his room he was never again seen. Some decomposed remains, supposed to be his, were afterward found in White River, but were not fully identified.

Grant Wilson, a colored man, who was known to be an important witness against some of the gang, was shot dead, in daylight, while walking from his home to Seymour. A Mr. McKinny, who was also a witness, was called to his door one night and shot dead. William Mower was murdered in a saloon row, but his murderers were never arrested. Pages could be filled with accounts of burglaries, robberies and thefts of all kinds, but more than enough has already been

Anarchy in the Heartland

told. Let the reader judge if the good citizens of Seymour were or were not justified in adopting the summary means they did to check this deluge of crime which they had tried in vain to check in any other way.

Let the reader judge, indeed. Before your mind is made up, there are many factors to consider.

Anarchy in the Heartland

The only known photograph of Val Elliott and Charles Roseberry supposedly taken May 8th, 1868 in Seymour. It was likely secured about the time that the photograph of John Reno and Frank Sparks had been taken. Elliott was about 22 years old and Roseberry was about 25 years old when they were hung.

The New Albany Jail, where Frank, Simeon and William Reno and Charles Anderson were hung.

Anarchy in the Heartland

The final resting place of Frank, William and Simeon Reno in Seymour's City Cemetery. The cemetery is located on land near the original Shields homestead.

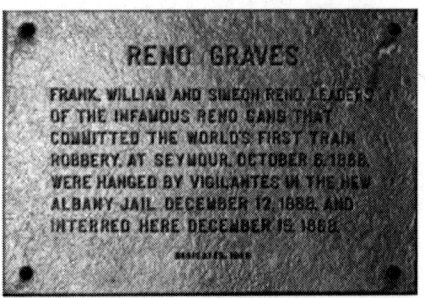

The marker in the foreground of the photograph above commemorates the world's first train robbery on October 6th, 1866, the hanging of the Renos on December 12, 1868 and their interment on December 15th, 1868. It was placed there in 1983. Also buried in the City Cemetery are the three Reno brother's parents, Wilk and Julia Reno as well Clint and John Reno.

Anarchy in the Heartland

Chapter 8: The Freethinker

In 1868, newspaper editorials were flooded with a nearly universal condemnation of the lynching of the Reno Gang members by vigilante mobs. Some of the roughest commentary came from the "enlightened" newspapers in the east. One account clearly lays the blame on the crude and lawless "White Trash" from Kentucky and Tennessee that had settled in Jackson County. Vitriol of this type was not uncommon in the press, but was usually reserved for southern whites still loyal to the Southern cause. This left little doubt that many outsiders felt Southern Indiana was "copperhead country" and merely an extension of the South.

The distant editorials demanded sharp responses from Jasper Monroe who continued to defend the lynching as a last resort taken by honest citizens when the Laws of the State had failed them. The irony here is Monroe was never a leading proponent of bigger government. Just the opposite was true. What this illustrates is Monroe's strong convictions to his own beliefs and his personal desire to change society as he saw fit. Monroe didn't want a bigger government to fix the problem. He wanted everyday citizens to take action in defiance of authority or the lack, thereof.

Monroe's primary career choice was Editor, rather than an MD. It was a perfect scenario for him to apply his true passion, social engineering. His

Anarchy in the Heartland

Freethinking, atheistic belief system was put on display weekly in print. Under the guise of writing to make people think, it went far beyond this. Monroe was impatient and wanted more than literary discourse. He wanted quick action to resolve the problems as he saw them. Monroe chose murder, not the legal system.

Lynching was the preferred method of capital punishment at the time as evidenced by the hanging of Mary Surratt, Lewis Powell, David Herold, and George Atzerodt on July 7th, 1865 for their part in the Lincoln assination. People saw that as just punishment and many felt it should have included several others including Samuel Mudd, Samuel Arnold, and Michael O'Laughlen. Monroe must have recognized that most in Indiana had accepted that "swinging from a rope" for one's crimes was far more than acceptable compared to a shot in the back, a cowardly deed. Monroe chose lynching as opposed to prearranged gun battles in the street. It was a logical, well thought-out choice in his mind.

Monroe lived at a time that was called the Golden Age of Freethinking. Freethinkers were self-described critical thinkers who sought to develop their own belief system through science, logic and reasoning. They would not accept conventional wisdom, authority or dogma that was imposed upon them by authorities. Freethinkers would neither immediately accept nor reject the authority imposed on them by others without proof and their own analysis. The founding of The Freethinkers Movement is thought to be those in

Anarchy in the Heartland

Europe opposed to the institution of the Church. It was very popular in Germany during the revolution of 1848 and many Germans that left for America brought this practice with them.

Freethinkers are still amongst us today with the modern name of "Skeptic". There are several organizations and publications, such as The Skeptical Inquirer, which embodies the practice of Freethinking. Organized Atheists are examples of Freethinkers as well as many authors, teachers and educators in nearly every institution in the country. Children today are exposed to Freethinking far more than those in Monroe's day. Freethinking may have diversified and changed names, but it is arguably far more widespread today that it was in 1868. It just happened to be that it was strongly focused in Seymour, Indiana.

One might not be able to connect a Freethinker with a vigilante lynching, but it is not too difficult to follow Monroe's logic. Monroe knew that Seymour had a problem because of its criminal activity. He also knew that the legal system was not only slow and cumbersome, but it was rife with corruption. He wrote about it many times, especially when events occurred that were not to his satisfaction. From Monroe's perspective, the legal system was defective and irrelevant by default. Crime had to end in Seymour to allow it and its citizens to become "enlightened". To change and move forward progressively out of what he most certainly viewed as the intellectual dark ages. Progress for society is what

Anarchy in the Heartland

fundamentally inspired Monroe and was the theme of the majority of his writings. Of course, it was progress as he personally defined it.

The "pulpit" of the newspaper was not enough to assure a counter-strike against the Reno's. For months, it was apparent that Monroe's calls for vigilante action were unheard. This must have been exceptionally frustrating to him. The power of his pen was not enough to motivate the citizens to take action. A direct organizing effort had to occur and it is likely Monroe began by simply walking to his neighbor's house next door.

One must pause at this point and consider what this may have meant. A Freethinker, by their own general definitions, is rooted in a personal belief system. Authority of any type is considered a potential enemy, so what made Monroe jump from Freethinking to wanting to organize others? The answer may lie in Monroe's exceptional frustration with the people of Seymour. No one had stepped forward to end the Reno's reign, as most were cowering behind locked doors in the evening, hoping to avoid their wrath.

Monroe could see no end to this. Despite his pleadings and literary rants to the contrary, Seymour residents took no action. For many, they regarded the Reno family as mischievous bad boys that had been dealt a bad hand in life unlike some of the wealthy elitists in their town. For some local people, they

Anarchy in the Heartland

personally knew the Renos and had very little negative to say about them. Monroe could see a stalemate and firmly believed the authority of the State had failed to correct the problem. Monroe wanted change and he wanted it quick.

Obsessed with change, he wrote to other area newspapers to avoid detection asking for vigilante action. This failed and he began to print vigilante posters under the names of The Seymour Vigilante Committee, The Jackson County Vigilance Society and the Southern Indiana Vigilante Committee. All had common themes and writing style and were most certainly the work of Jasper Monroe. The most famous of the 1868 vigilante posters, signed as the Southern Indiana Vigilance Committee states the following:

HEADQUARTERS SOUTHERN INDIANA, VIGILANCE COMMITTEE.

TO THE PEOPLE OF THE UNITED STATES!

"SALUS POPULI SUPREMA LEX"

WHEREAS, it became necessary for this organization to meet out summary punishment to the leaders of the thieves, robbers, murderers and desperadoes, who for many years defied law and order, and threatened the lives and property of honest citizens of this portion of Indiana, and as the late fearful tragedy at New Albany testifies that justice is slow, but sure, we promulgate this our prouncuamenta,

Anarchy in the Heartland

for the purpose of justifying to the world, and particularly to the people of the State of Indiana, and future action which we may take.

We deeply deplore the necessity which called our organization into existencel but the laws of our state were so defective that as they now stand on the Statute Books, they all favor criminals going unwhipt of justice; a retrospective view will show that in this respect we speak only the truth.

Having first lopped off the branches, and finally uprooted the tree of evil which was in our midst, in defiance of us and our laws, we beg to be allowed to rest here, and be not forced again to take the law into our own hands. We are very loth to shed blood again, and will not do so unless compelled in defence of our lives.

A WARNING

We are all well aware that at the present time, a combination of the few remaining thieves, their friends and sympathizers, has been formed against us, all have threatened all kinds of vengeance against persons whom they suppose to belong to this organization. They threaten assassination in every form, and that they will commit arson in such ways as to defy legal detection. The carrying out in whole, or in part, of each or any of these designs, is the only thing that will again cause us to rise in our own defence. The following named persons are solemnly warned, that

Anarchy in the Heartland

their designs and opinions are known, and that they cannot, unknown to us, make a move toward retaliation.

Wilk Reno, Clinton Reno, Trick Reno, James Greer, Stephen Greer, Fee Johnson, Chris. Price, Harvey Needham, Meade Fislar, Mart Lowe, Rolland Lee, William Sparks, Jesse Thompson, William Hate, William Biggars, James Fislar, Pollard Able.

If the above named individuals desire to remain in our midst, to pursue honest callings, and otherwise conduct themselves as law abiding citizens, we will protect them always. - If however, they commence their devilish designs against us, our property, or any good citizen of this district, we will rise but once more; do not trifle with us; for if you do, we will follow you to the bitter end; and give you a "short shrift and a hempen collar." As to this, our actions in the past, will be a guarantee for our conduct in the future.

We trust this will have a good effect. We repeat, we are very loth again to take life, and hope we shall never more be necessitated to take the law into our own hands.

Dec. 21. 1868
By order of the Committee.

Warning published by the Southern Indiana Vigilance Committee

Anarchy in the Heartland

The posters, likely spread by railway workers during their normal runs had the desired affect. It began to unite a group of people in Seymour with a common interest, to remove the threat of further train robberies by removing the Renos. Remember, the Renos had not robbed local banks, only sporadically hit local businesses and murdered no one and their family while they were sleeping in their homes. The single biggest threat the Reno Gang represented was the disruption of rail service. The Adams Express Company and the Railroad Companies were responsible for the loss of stolen money.

Monroe lived on Chestnut Street in Seymour with his family, servants and apprentice printers. Next to him were several families of railroad employees. Monroe must have recognized the opportunity to align with like-minded individuals, perhaps fresh from Germany, who could have easily had a similar belief system. Monroe was also reported to have been fluent in German.

The railroaders presented the muscle that would be needed for the retribution that occurred. The older and weaker citizens of Seymour would not have directly confronted the Reno Gang, even if the citizens were facing shackled prisoners. Throwing people onto wagons, pitching a rope over tree branches, slipping the noose over a struggling prisoner and hauling away a flatbed wagon was the work of younger men. Younger men, that would have been easy to mobilize, who did not have to come in from

Anarchy in the Heartland

the remote farmlands of Jackson County and could have been available on short notice. The railroad employees of Seymour, by deductive reasoning, certainly compromised the muscle needed to lynch the Reno gang.

Other authors have failed to connect Monroe directly with the vigilance committee other than making a "lynch law" call through the Seymour Times. Understanding Dr. Jasper R. Monroe was certainly not an easy task, but following him through his later years will help make the job easier.

Following the killings of the Reno Gang, relative peace was restored to Seymour, but Monroe's work was not finished. He continued to write about the relative evils of Christianity and correspond with other like minded people across the country for the next decade. In 1878, he went to Watkins Glen, New York in what was to be remembered as the first National Freethinkers Convention. According to George E Macdonald's "Fifty Years of Freethought" written in 1929, some of the notable attendees were:

"A list of speakers and attendants, actual and announced, at the Watkins, N.Y., Freethinkers' convention held in August, 1878, shows Who was Who in the Liberal ranks fifty years ago:

Hon. Geo. W. Julian, Indiana.
James Parton, Massachusetts.
Hon. Frederick Douglas, Washington, D.C.

Anarchy in the Heartland

Dr. J.M. Peebles, New Jersey.
Elder F.W. Evans, Mt. Lebanon, N.Y.
Parker Pillsbury, Concord, N.H.
Hon. Elizur Wright, Boston.
Prof. J.E. Oliver, Ithaca, N.Y.
Hon. judge E.P. Hurlbut, Albany, N.Y.
Horace Seaver, editor of The Investigator.
J.P. Mendum, publisher of The Investigator.
D.M. Bennett, editor of The Truth Seeker.
Col. John C. Bundy, editor of The Religio-Philosophical Journal.
G.L. Henderson, editor of The Positive Thinker.
Asa K. Butts, editor Evolution.
M.J.R. Hargrave, editor of The Freethought Journal.
G.A. Loomis, editor of The Shaker.
Benj R. Tucker, editor of The Word.
Dr. J.R. Monroe, editor of The Seymour Times.
C.D.B. Mills, Syracuse.
Mrs. Matilda Joselyn Gage, corresponding secretary of the National Woman Suffrage Association.
Mrs. Clara Neyman, New York City.
Giles B. Stebbins , Detroit, Mich.
Charles Ellis, Boston.
William S. Bell, New Bedford, Mass.
Rev. A.B. Bradford, Pennsylvania.
Thaddeus B. Wakeman, New York City.
Dr, T.L. Brown, Binghatuton, N.Y.
Rev. J.H. Horton, Auburn, N.Y.

Anarchy in the Heartland

Prof. J.H.W. Toohey, Chelsea, Mass.
Prof. A.L. Rawson, New York City.
Rev. William Ellery, Copeland, Neb.
T.C. Leland, New York City.
Ella E. Gibson, Barre, Mass.
Dr. J.L. York, California.
Mrs. Lucy A. Colman, Syracuse.
Mrs. P.R. Lawrence, Quincy, Mass.
Mrs. Grace L. Parkhurst, Elkland, Pa.
Hudson Tuttle, Berlin Heights, Ohio.
Rev. O.B. Frothingham, New York.
Mrs. Elizabeth Cady Stanton, New Jersey.
The Hutchinson Family, singers.

And the names of Liberal lecturers not included in the list were

Charles Orchardson, New. York.
Ingersoll Lockwood, New York.
B.F. Underwood, Thorndike, Mass.
Prof. William Denton, Wellesley, Mass.
W.F. Jamieson, Albion, Mich.
E.C. Walker, Florence, Iowa.
C. Fannie Allyn, Stoneham, Mass.
Moses Hull, Boston.
Laura Kendrick, Boston.
Mrs. Augusta Cooper Bristol, Vineland, N.J.
J.W. Stillman, New York.
Dr. A.J. Clark, Indianapolis.
D.W. Hull, Michigan.
C.L. James, Wisconsin."

Anarchy in the Heartland

Monroe was probably in Watkins Glen pitching his 1875 manuscript titled "Dramas and miscellaneous poems", but another individual earned himself some international press coverage. De Robigne Mortimer Bennett, better known as D. M. Bennett, was arrested for selling a copy of "Cupids Yoke and the Holy Scriptures: in a letter", a banned "indecent, licentious, and lewd" work written by Parker Pillsbury. Supposedly, Bennett simply had the book on the table while the author was temporarily away. The authorities were not buying it and Bennett was convicted in 1879 and served 13 months hard labor. 200,000 people signed a petition for his release, to no avail.

Monroe was certainly not the stature of Frederick Douglas, the famous black abolitionist in attendance, but nonetheless had aligned himself with many significant intellectuals of his time. Most people in the Freethought movement were atheists or agnostics, but other history makers at this convention would lead a charge for Minority and Women's Rights. Monroe's writings were primarily cerebral poetry, atheistic in nature and may not have garnered special notoriety amongst his peers since there were many others with similar scripts. When recalling Monroe's "Ode to Brownstown" poem, it's certainly possible others would have considered his poetry to be somewhat lacking.

Whether the arrest of Bennett selling lewd material in Watkins Glen had any impact on Seymour

Anarchy in the Heartland

residents is not known, but 1878 became a turning point for Monroe in Seymour. By 1880, he would no longer be the editor of a newspaper though he still lived there on posh Chestnut Street with his family and servants. One could argue that he simply overstayed his welcome, times had changed, or that Monroe felt he was getting nowhere fast a sleepy, backwater town of Seymour far outside the intellectual mainstream.

In 1881, he moved to Indianapolis and took the Seymour Times with him; meaning all the assets and equipment the company owned. He began publishing a monthly national magazine called the "Iron-Clad Age" which had nothing to do with warships. It was a new Freethinkers magazine firmly rooted in atheism and had a national circulation of some 7,000 readers. His next published manuscript was written in 1882 and was titled "Holy Bible stories; Modern rendition of some ancient fables". In retrospect, it's probable that his opinions were no longer welcomed in Seymour and this hastened his departure in 1881. He no longer had a local audience to write for.

Monroe continued his prolific writing and correspondence with many others across the country. The Iron-Clad Age" was perhaps his lifetime dream. Fighting against authority, more specifically the authority of the church was Monroe's calling, not surgery. So how could a devout atheist become involved with the lynching of the Reno Gang?

Anarchy in the Heartland

The ultimate authority in Monroe's life was Jasper R Monroe. There was no law, church or state that usurped his critical thinking. Once he had decided that Seymour could not progress with the Renos there, they had to be eliminated. Killing the Renos would send no one to hell, for there was none. The same scenario applies to the Indiana judicial system in Monroe's mind. Therefore, the Southern Indiana Vigilance Committee was in response to, and far exceeded the Reno Gang's reign of anarchy. Most likely, the architect and spiritual leader of the vigilante mob was Dr. Jasper R. Monroe, surgeon, editor, publisher, poet, Freethinker and devout Atheist.

Anarchy in the Heartland

Famous cartoon titled "Copperhead Party" that appeared in Harper's Magazine February 28th, 1863. Southern Indiana was considered a region of backwoods, southern sympathizers and worse by many elitist eastern newspapers.

A photograph from the Library of Congress. The Lincoln conspirators were publicly hung on July 7th, 1865. In the atmosphere of this retribution, the vigilantes of Jackson County must have felt emboldened and justified. All they needed was a zealous leader.

Anarchy in the Heartland

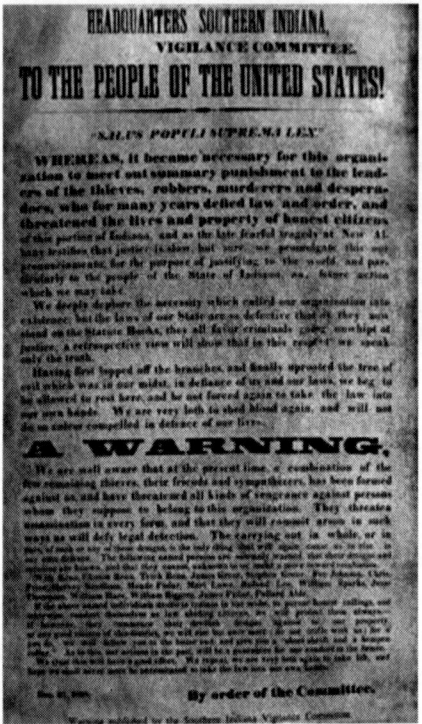

This reproduction poster closely resembles the original vigilante poster circulating throughout southern Indiana just after the Reno Gang was hung. The original was produced on a printing press and contained several different font type sizes. There were few places an underground movement could have had these printed in 1868. Monroe's newspaper was one of them.

Anarchy in the Heartland

Chapter 9: Fanning the Flames

The town of Rockford had been dissolving around the Renos and Jasper Monroe in the mid 1850s. While the Renos saw their town disappearing, Monroe saw his livelihood disappear. In fact, the demise of Rockford had a catalyst; the unexplained fires that swept away many homes and businesses. Most considered this to be the work of the Renos, who supposedly wanted cheap real estate. But there were two other possibilities for the arsons.

Meedy Shields' new enterprise had not yet secured the northbound train stop and depot in Seymour. All the way until 1857, the J, M & I railroad continued to load and unload passengers and goods in Rockford. Shields had plans to introduce the railroad stopping Bill into the Indiana Legislature at the time, but there were no guarantee it would quickly pass. This begs the question, could Shields' or any of his business partners or family been responsible for the fires of Rockford? Certainly aggressive capitalists have been known to bribe authorities and bend the rules, but burning out competitive businesses was another matter altogether.

When examining the Seymour ruling class of the 1850s, you had an aging Meedy Shields, his two sons, William and Lycurgus. There was also Travis Carter, who invested heavily in his own woodworking business and related properties. There was John Blish's Mill, who was Shield's son-in-law, plus a

Anarchy in the Heartland

handful of minor storeowners including dry goods merchants, saloon owners and railroad employees. While the temptation was certainly there, these people must have realized that the demise of Rockford was a forgone conclusion without any significant actions of their own. Burning Rockford to the ground might destroy a competitor or perhaps generate some reconstruction business, but it is doubtful that any of these individuals would have risked all they had accumulated to torch Rockford. Besides, the booming town of Seymour would have kept them very distracted in running their growing businesses.

The other "candidate" for the burning of Rockford besides the Renos and the Seymour merchants was "by parties unknown". Parties unknown could not have been members of the Reno Gang, for in the 1850s there were none. The Civil War crime connections the Renos made would come during and after the war. In effect, there was no Reno Gang in the 1850s, only the Renos themselves. Would they burn the town to buy cheap real estate? Real estate purchased for what purpose? There is no doubt that Wilkes Reno saw an opportunity and squandered the family money he had inherited to buy up the property, but there was no obvious plan to rebuild Rockford. No plan to turn the town into farmland. There simply was no strong motivation by Wilkes or his sons to burn down Rockford.

According to the History of Jackson County written in 1886:

Anarchy in the Heartland

"The railroad company built a large and fine depot, and Mr. Kester a large pork house beside it. On the railroad and on the corner just north were large two-story buildings used for whisky shops. Frank Able built a hotel and kept a bar and sold beer, never known in the county until the railroad reached it.

All the buildings named were, a few years later, burned down by incendiaries. Not a vestige remains of many of them. Other small houses have been erected in their stead.

Rockford Lodge of Odd Fellows had joined with J. P. Fentress in building a, store, with a hall above. This stood on the north end of a lot belonging to the late Alfred Miller. It, too, was destroyed by fire.

The only church ever owned by Old or New Rockford, stood on the outskirts of the old town, not far from the old water-tank, on the railroad. It was long ago set on fire and burned down. We believe it belonged to the Methodists."

From this account, the Methodist Church appears to be one of the first victims of arson, well before the businesses.

Incredulous and counterintuitive as it may be, Dr Jasper R Monroe was a perfect arson suspect. Although he apparently had much to lose in the burning of Rockford, did he not recognize that Seymour would become the ultimate victor over

Anarchy in the Heartland

Rockford? It's likely that Monroe and Shields had been talking for years about the move of the Rockford Herald to Seymour. Monroe was a shrewd businessman and certainly knew that Rockford would eventually lose the battle. He also knew that the Renos or some rogue Seymour merchants would be blamed for starting the fires. Building a bigger and better paper in Seymour would be easier if Rockford was wiped off the map. But there was another caveat.

Monroe was certainly an educated intellectual with radical ideas on Society, Church and State. He generally ignored his medical practice to become involved in social engineering practices. The power of his words could change the world in his mind. But initially, they did not. All of his poetry and articles had a limited effect on his readership. For Monroe, this could have been the ultimate act of betrayal. Perhaps he viewed himself as the Pied Piper of New Age Reasoning and he was having trouble motivating these "backwoods" locals to progress to a new enlightenment.

Monroe must have felt exceeding frustrated at this. Some of his earlier writings in Rockford reported the results of cock fighting. This was no topic and vocation for a man who considered himself an intellectual giant and motivator of men. It was an insult to his dignity. These small town stooges had no interest in his enlightened reasoning. They were too busy betting on cockfights, local elections, getting drunk and talking about various get-rich-quick schemes.

Anarchy in the Heartland

Heathens, god-fearing, superstitious, lazy, inept heathens surrounded Monroe. He must have been furious his intellect was being wasted.

Change had to occur. The pot had to be stirred. Significant events needed to happen in order to make the people listen to him. The fires of Rockford would provide a galvanizing series of events that would make people turn to him and read his newspaper. Monroe was leaving town anyway. He would not be a likely suspect. Townspeople would gladly turn to him to get the latest crime information and gossip. He would control the information with an iron fist and be the only source to get the facts out to the people. Monroe also knew that between crises, he could pepper his growing newspaper with enlightened reasoning and society could eventually change for the better, if they would only listen to him.

Perhaps not surprisingly, Seymour began to experience a series of unexplained fires after Monroe's move to Seymour. Again, in the History of Jackson County regarding Seymour:

"This town's progress being rapid, and its population increasing apace, several other rooms were rented throughout the town for school purposes, between 1853, when this house was built, and 1860, when the first national census of the town was taken, which showed a population of 924. The old school building was destroyed by fire June 9, 1859, and a new,

Anarchy in the Heartland

two-story brick school building was at once erected on the lot now occupied by John Sansterer's residence."

And some years later a much larger fire:

"The church of this denomination was built in 1866 on a lot lying directly south of the planing-mill, now owned by T. Carter & Co. The church was built of brick, at a cost of $4,000. This building was destroyed by fire in 1879, when Carter & Co.'s planing-mill was burned."

The reports of the day seem to indicate the fire originated in Carter's woodworking operation, but one should consider whether the church was the original target as was the old schoolhouse. Both were institutions of authority. Authority that Monroe may have taken issue with. Again the fires could have helped focus readers on Monroe's intellectual wisdom. There were no other significant fires reported after 1879 in the 1886 book.

There were other troubling events that occurred besides the fires and the lynching of the Reno Gang members. One of them was the killing of Moore Woodmansee in 1866. This murder was unique from several angles. First, the Reno Gang members loitering around the Rader House typically preyed on transients, people from the outside just passing through. Woodmansee was from nearby Medora and his family was well known in the area. His grandfather had been an early pioneer, his father a noted farmer

Anarchy in the Heartland

and his uncle owned the dry goods store in Seymour. He was a very well recognized citizen of Jackson County.

No doubt he was robbed on the evening he died, but what was the cause of the murder? More importantly, what motivated the killers to drag the body out of town to the White River and behead the corpse? No one saw Woodmansee leave town for Rockford on the White River. Perhaps it was something Woodmansee did or saw? Wouldn't a robbery victim simply been knocked unconscious as many had been? What does the beheading tell us about the murder?

The mistreatment of any corpse was meant to send a powerful message. It could also generate a powerful response. The beheading of Woodmansee was a cold, ruthless act of violence certain to elicit an equally violent reaction. Up until that time, Monroe appeared to have trouble motivating people to form the vigilante committee. A significant, deplorable event had to occur. The Moore Woodmansee murder fits the bill. Here is one possible scenario regarding the robbing and killing of this young man from Medora.

Woodmansee found himself wandering the streets of Seymour after an evening of drinking and carousing. It was late. He was set upon by thugs who robbed him at gun or knifepoint then pistol whipped or clubbed him into unconsciousness. He was left lying in a yard or back alley. Woodmansee regained

Anarchy in the Heartland

consciousness and required help. He needed a doctor. He was bleeding and disoriented. There was no immediate care center and no hospital to go to. He made his way or someone lead him to a doctor in town. Dr Jasper Monroe.

As difficult as this is to fathom, consider that beheading an individual not only takes time, it requires the proper equipment. Your average robber might carry a pocketknife, but wouldn't have the best tools to cut through layers of flesh and bone. But a surgeon would, a surgeon like Dr Monroe.

Consider for a moment what the killing of Woodmansee represented. It was the first time an innocent local man had been robbed and murdered. It was brutally committed, designed to elicit a strong response. What robber would take the time to move the body, running a risk of drawing unwanted attention? Take the body two miles away and then dump it in the river? Why not bury the body if the killer had this much time?

The newspaper reports said Woodmansee disappeared in Seymour, not Rockford. Where was the evidence that any member of the Reno Gang had done anything like this before? They had not according to most accounts. Woodmansee's grisly murder and mutilation must have been designed for pure shock value. The body's discovery certainly invoked people's wrath and helped set the stage for the vigilante action that Monroe had first called for in 1865.

The scenario involving Monroe is certainly possible, but had never been discussed or written about openly. Monroe was obviously a Freethinker and had anarchistic tendencies, but was he a psychopathic arsonist and killer?

Anarchy in the Heartland

This is the image drawn by James Flanders, engineer on the botched train robbery attempt near Brownstown, Indiana. He said it was used to signal other vigilantes that an event would take place. Flanders said this symbol appeared on barns and fences just prior to the first hanging. This information appeared in an article by the Cincinnati Enquirer newspaper and later in the "Masked Halters" book by Edwin Boley.

The modern symbol for Anarchy recognized throughout the world today.

Anarchy in the Heartland

Chapter 10: Let the Reader be the Judge

There is little doubt that many have celebrated the "American Dream" created by Meedy Shields. He was undoubtedly an extremely driven individual and knew how to craft a fortune for himself in a time when most Americans were simply struggling to survive. This was a time when the country had only an upper and lower class. This caste system would be in effect for decades to come. Using political insight and leverage, he forged a business empire and let little stand in his way. One could argue that this is the true essence of Capitalism.

When a select few accumulate wealth, there are consequences. These are not measured on any corporate spreadsheets; the unintended consequence of small towns disappearing and the livelihoods of their people with them. Literally hundreds of people were displaced when Seymour was created. Many people left Indiana for new horizons, others stayed. Those who stayed had a choice of whether to join the new enterprises of Seymour, run by a select few individuals, or find other ways of making a living.

The Renos took the low road. They made a brief attempt to relocate further west, but returned to their roots in Jackson County. During this excursion and during the Civil War, they must have felt used, betrayed and destined to remain at the bottom of the American caste system. Those giving speeches and leading parades to entice young men to join the war

Anarchy in the Heartland

effort was none other than those who controlled the town of Seymour and its fortunes. The Renos perhaps saw themselves as cannon fodder, doing the fighting and heavy lifting for the elitist rich.

No one can justify becoming a criminal, stealing and murdering, but when wealth is tightly held and controlled, this will always be the unintended consequence. When little hope or sharing of wealth occurs, the "peasants" will always revolt. History will repeat itself time and time again. In the mid to late 1860s, this is exactly what happened in Seymour.

However, Jackson County reacted far differently to the crime wave around them. Rather than turning to the legal system, the "good citizens" turned to violent crime themselves. Some argue it was far more despicable than anything the Renos had ever done; mass murder. While no one can justify the Reno crime empire, no one can justify the lynching of three brothers and several others.

Considering Jackson County people were no different from average Americans at the time, something was unique about the local situation. That "something" was simply induced mass hysteria. Jasper Monroe successfully painted a dire and imminent danger to everyone. People became fearful of their own lives and property when the chances of them being a victim of crime was probably nil. The Renos had a taste for bank cash carried on trains, not a stash under anyone's mattress.

Anarchy in the Heartland

The panic crafted by Monroe and gleefully endorsed by leading citizens was what made Jackson County unique to this day. Consider Monroe's methodology carefully. This was far more than scare tactics to gain attention and sell newspapers. It was a call to action. Literally, it was a call to murder fellow citizens and become the judge, jury and executioner. The failure to act would have meant imminent danger and a real possibility of becoming a victim of theft, rape or murder.

Monroe was an Anarchist. He was one of the first of his kind, along with Robert G Ingersoll, to organize in America in the mid to late 19th century under the name of Freethinkers. There was more than Free Thought involved in the Freethinkers Movement, there was also a call to action by many. The unintended consequences of Shield's empire provided fertile grounds for an Anarchist like Monroe. In his mind, the people are the law. There is no law above the people. There is no government, religion, business or entity that usurps the law of the people. Recalling the Latin phrase on the printed 1868 Vigilante Poster:

"SALUS POPULI SUPREMA LEX"

Salus populi suprema lex esto "Let the good of the people be the supreme law" or "The welfare of the people shall be the supreme law". Doctors were well versed in Latin.

Anarchy in the Heartland

Whatever one thinks of Capitalism, Freethought or its cousin, the Socialist Movement of about the same time, it took more than simple ideological differences to create one of the bloodiest and cruel chapters in American history. The events in rural Jackson County in the Heartland of the United States are seldom written about, not to mention discussed in academia.

Perhaps it's the lack of understanding of the dynamics of the situation or the less-than-famous region it occupied then, as it is now. There was very little glamour in the harsh conditions in the Midwest at the time. We still tend to focus our attention on the urbanized east or west coast. So much of the history of America is contained within the land between, yet so few lessons are gleaned from them. On the other hand, perhaps the lack of discussion is obvious shame.

Capitalism built the heartland, but not without unintended consequences. These were often dealt with harshly and without compassion. The "have not's" turned towards crime. Bloodthirsty vigilante mobs made up of ordinary people roamed the countryside plotting their next revenge. The state and local government was powerless, distracted or disinterested. Total Anarchy reigned. Local society, in effect, had broken down for nearly a decade.

Today, Capitalism is as strong as ever, as are the unintended consequences when wealth is horded. Millions of ordinary citizens still turn to criminal

Anarchy in the Heartland

activities as an escape or attack on the "haves". Also, millions of ordinary citizens could still be waiting for the next Jasper Monroe to invoke violence as a defense against a well-crafted threat against them. In some respects, we have not progressed as a society, for the same mistakes are being made.

As you, the reader, ponder the events of this haze-filled, distant past in America, consider where America is headed and where you have staked your claim. Will you follow Shields' example as a business and political leader without knowledge or consideration of unintended consequences? Will you assume the role of the Renos and take what you can, when you can and how you can? Perhaps you will choose to become an activist such as Monroe and become a pied-piper for whatever cause you choose. Will you invoke fear as a recruitment tool? And will you demand a call to action rather than encourage additional thought? Will you blindly follow as did the semi-organized mob of killers who lynched the Reno Gang?

These simple questions might take a lifetime of experiences and knowledge for you to be able to answer. Regardless, take your time when you make these decisions. Learn of other little-know examples of societal de-evolution often hidden from our classrooms or media outlets. In fact, you are challenged to be your own Freethinker, and unlike Monroe, this book gives you no particular call to action other than to think about your decisions in life.

Anarchy in the Heartland

Perhaps this is a time for a more distant text to be considered.

"It is proper for you, Kalamas [the people of the village of Kesaputta], to doubt, to be uncertain; uncertainty has arisen in you about what is doubtful. Come, Kalamas. Do not go upon what has been acquired by repeated hearing; nor upon tradition; nor upon rumor; nor upon what is in a scripture; nor upon surmise; nor upon an axiom; nor upon specious reasoning; nor upon a bias towards a notion that has been pondered over; nor upon another's seeming ability; nor upon the consideration, 'The monk is our teacher.' Kalamas, when you yourselves know: 'These things are bad; these things are blameable; these things are censured by the wise; undertaken and observed, these things lead to harm and ill, abandon them.

"...Do not accept anything by mere tradition... Do not accept anything just because it accords with your scriptures... Do not accept anything merely because it agrees with your pre-conceived notions... But when you know for yourselves—these things are moral, these things are blameless, these things are praised by the wise, these things, when performed and undertaken, conduce to well-being and happiness—then do you live acting accordingly." - the Buddha, from the text Kalama Sutta

Anarchy in the Heartland

From the book "Thomas Paine" by John E Remsburg Monroe wrote this glowing tribute: "With the wand of his genius he turned aside the scroll that concealed the future of our country, and by the inspiring picture he thus presented our disheartened and hard-pressed forefathers were nerve to press forward, to brave every peril, to dare every danger, to defy every death, till tyranny was throttled and man was free". Thomas Paine was an English-born revolutionary, radical, inventor, and intellectual. He lived and worked in Britain until age 37, when he emigrated to the British American colonies, in time to participate in the American Revolution. He became notorious because of The Age of Reason (1793-94), the book advocating deism and arguing against Christian doctrines. In France, he also wrote the pamphlet Agrarian Justice (1795), discussing the origins of property, and introduced the concept of a guaranteed minimum income.

Anarchy in the Heartland

George Washington Julian was a member of Congress representing the 4^h and 5^h Districts in Indiana, a Liberal Republican like Monroe and a prolific author.

The famous orator, author, abolitionist and statesman had also been a headliner at Monroe's Freethought convention in Watkins Glen, New York.

Anarchy in the Heartland

From the Freethought Trail, this is the site of the infamous 1878 Freethinkers convention in Watkins Glen, New York. These conventions were notable for the number of important figures involved, such as Robert G. Ingersoll and C.D.B. Mills. However, the first convention, in 1878, is especially important because it is the site where D.M. Bennett was arrested for selling a banned text known as "Cupid's Yokes".

A woman named Josephine Tilton left her bookstand for a short time and asked Bennett to take care of it. While she was gone, someone purchased "Cupid's Yokes" from Bennett. He was later arrested and sentenced to serve 13 months of hard labor in prison, and pay a $300 fine. The result of the trial was very unpopular; the decision was criticized by all nonreligious press, and a petition for a pardon for Bennett had more than 200,000 signatures on it before being sent to President Hayes. Despite this petition and a letter from Robert G. Ingersoll asking for a pardon, Bennett was forced to serve his full sentence. Dr. Jasper Monroe from Seymour was in attendance.

Anarchy in the Heartland

Hollywood cashed in on the Reno Gang saga by releasing "Rage at Dawn" in 1955 with Indiana native Forrest Tucker portraying Frank Reno. Elvis Presley made his movie debut playing "Honest" Clint Reno in the 1956 movie titled "Love Me Tender". Both movies were highly fictionalized and few historical facts were presented. In 1939 and 1944, Robert Shields, a distant relative of Meedy Shields, wrote two books on the Renos and was convinced Hollywood "borrowed" his work without giving him the proper credit. Robert Shields was a former minister and English teacher who was best known for leaving behind a 37.5 million word diary about everyday mundane events that occurred during his lifetime. Shields' two books were based on the autobiography of John Reno written in 1879, which Reno failed to find a market for. Suffice it to say that Hollywood made more money on the Reno story than any of the participants or authors that followed. Unfortunately, the stories were pure fiction.

Anarchy in the Heartland

Epilog

Jasper Monroe, who coincidently used the name Jesse and James during his lifetime, set up the "Iron-Clad Age" as a weekly publication at 55 Indiana Avenue near downtown Indianapolis. This publication was a vanity press for his poetry and atheistic belief system. Never once was he publically questioned for his role in the vigilante movement in Jackson County, though many suspected the good doctor of leading the way.

He corresponded with a diverse group of people throughout the years. One was David Overmyer, who was raised in Jackson County and went on to attend Depaw University in Greencastle, Indiana and later, politics in Kansas. Several of his letters are included in the David Overmyer papers housed at Kansas State University. Some of Monroe's last letters to Overmyer complained about his failing health.

The Indiana Historical Society has the Reuben H. Power collection. Power married Monroe's daughter Lula and helped his publish the "Iron-Clad Age" Reuben Power served on the gunboat "Somerset" a wooden-hulled, side-wheeled ferryboat. It was commissioned in 1862 and served in the Civil War during the iron clad age of the Monitor and the Virginia (Merrimack). Its pretty obvious Monroe took the name for his publication from his son-in-law's experience serving on an older-technology wooden boat in an iron clad age.

Anarchy in the Heartland

Monroe's best know published titles were mainly poetry and booklets which included "The Origin of Man; or, the early reformers: a tale of tails" written about 1881, "Holy Bible Stories: modern rendition of some ancient fables" written in 1882 and "Genesis Revised: Revision of Genesis I-II-III; only authentic history of creation" written in 1891. It's obvious that an atheist in America found many cold shoulders in the 1800s as they often do today. Monroe never found a wide audience for way of thinking and never seemed to gain national acceptance amongst his peers.

It's more than likely his health suffered from alcohol abuse yet he filed for a war pension for rheumatism but was declined. He later reapplied and finally received his pension despite only serving a few months in the service. His medical practice was poorly documented despite the title he received from the Kentucky School of Medicine near Louisville. He only attended one year; 1858. This was 8 years after arriving in Rockford from Monmouth County, New Jersey where he was born.

Monroe died in Indianapolis on November 9th, 1891 at the age of 68 and was buried in the large and prestigious Crown Hill Cemetery. Crown Hill is the final resting place of a variety of notables including President Benjamin Harrison, Booth Tarkington, James Whitcomb Riley, famous gun maker Dr Richard J Gatling, drug company founder Colonel Eli Lilly, famous car makers the Duesenberg brothers,

Anarchy in the Heartland

several Indiana Governors and Congressmen including Oliver P Morton and George Washington Julian. Last, but not least, was the famous Indiana gangster John Dillinger.

Anarchy in the Heartland

Indianapolis was a welcome home for Freethinkers and in the early 1850s, a number of Germans called the Forty-eighters moved to the city. Many of them were political activists who had been persecuted in their homeland or were disillusioned with German politics. The revolution of 1848 had not brought about the liberal social and political changes they'd hoped for in Germany, so they came to America. The first organization established by the Forty-eighters in Indianapolis was the Turnverein. Some of the more radical members of the Forty-eighters and Turners were freethinkers. They founded the Freethinkers Society of Indianapolis in 1870 to promote freethought ideas.

Author Kurt Vonnegut's great-grandfather, Clemens Vonnegut, was the first president of the organization. He was a well-respected businessman in the community and a member of the Indianapolis Public School board for many years. The group fought against religion in the schools and started a Freethinker's Sunday School. Today, the facility is known as the Athenaeum.

Anarchy in the Heartland

From the Council for Secular Humanism, Robert Green Ingersoll entered public life as a Peoria, Illinois, attorney. Following distinguished service in the Civil War, he served as the first Attorney General of Illinois. Politically, he allied with the Republicans, the party of Lincoln and in those days the voice of progressivism. "A.J. Tomlinson: Plainfolk Modernist" by R. G. Robins called Jasper Monroe a Robert Ingersoll-style rationalist. Tomlinson was a leading figure in the Pentecostal movement and apparently had no love for Monroe's "Iron-Clad Age".

Anarchy in the Heartland

Gun-seller and Gun-slinger Gatling and Dillinger's memorials at Crown Hill Cemetery in Indianapolis, Indiana. These two photographs illustrate both the capitalist and criminal, not unlike the Shields and Reno families.

Anarchy in the Heartland

Image Credits – not cited in captions

National Archives, Washington, DC

Library of Congress, Washington, DC

United States Patent and Trademark Office, Washington, DC

Various non-copyrighted or public domain images older than 100 years

The author's personal collection

Anarchy in the Heartland

Bibliography – Chronological

Chandler & Co.; *Business Directory for Indiana: Seymour Businesses and Owners*; 1868

Brant & Fuller; *Reno Gang: History of Jackson County, Indiana*; 1886

Moffett, Cleveland; *The Destruction of the Reno Gang: Stories from the Archives of the Pinkerton Detective Agency*; McClure's Magazine; 1895

Rowan, Richard Wilmer; *A Family of Outlaws*; 1931

Shields, Robert; *Seymour, Indiana and the famous story of the Reno gang: Who terrorized America with the first train robberies in world*; 1939; ASIN B00089LL7E

Shields, Robert; *Illustrations for Mules Crossing,: A history of the Reno era; the story of the Reno brothers*; 1944; ASIN B0007HS6HU

Volland, Robert Frederick; *The Reno Gang of Seymour*; 1948; LCCN 48021348

Bogardus, Carl Robert; *The Scarlet Mask, or, The Story of the Notorious Reno Gang*; 1960; ASIN B0007I0CF8

Anarchy in the Heartland

Hogg, Wilgus Wade; *The First Train Robbery*; 1977; LCCN 77-73272

Boley, Edwin J.; *The Masked Halters*; 1977; ASIN B0006CZCIC

Jackson County Historical Society; *John Reno: The world's first train robber and self proclaimed leader of the infamous Reno Gang, Seymour, Indiana by John Reno*; 1879; reprinted with annotations 1993; ASIN B0006P2G5G

Lucas, Todd; *The Story of the Reno Gang*; 1996; Franklin College, Indiana Videotape Library

Jackson County Historical Society; *Tragic Destiny - Demise of the Reno Gang by Loren W Noblitt*; 2000

Lewis, John M, III; *The Reno story : the world's first train robbers, the facts--the fictions--the legends*; 2003; Graessle-Mercer; ASIN: B0006P7AXO

Seymour Museum, Seymour Indiana; *Saving Seymour Stories by Charlotte A Sellers*; 2007